Copyright © 2024 Ivo Bernardo

All rights reserved. This book or any portion thereof may not be reproduced or used in any manner whatsoever without the express written permission of the publisher except for the use of brief quotations in a book review.

Cover art by Laura Deus (lauradeus.com)

First Printing, 2024

ISBN 9798320570006

Ivo Bernardo

1. INTRODUCTION	**5**
2. SETTING UP MYSQL	**7**
2.1. INSTALLING MYSQL SERVER, SHELL AND WORKBENCH	9
2.2. LAUNCHING MYSQL SERVICE FROM SCRATCH	27
2.3. GETTING FAMILIAR WITH MYSQL WORKBENCH	29
2.4. SETTING UP THE SAKILA DATABASE	37
3. QUERY BASICS	**46**
3.1 QUERY INTRODUCTION AND COLUMN FILTERING	46
3.2 WHERE STATEMENTS	50
3.3 NEW COLUMNS AND CALCULATIONS	58
3.4 ADDITIONAL QUERY CLAUSES	67
3.5 EXERCISE SECTION	79
3.5.1 EXERCISES	79
3.5.2 EXERCISE SOLUTIONS	80
4. SQL DATA TYPES	**81**
4.1. NUMERIC DATA TYPES	84
4.2. TEXT DATA TYPES	89
4.3. DATE DATA TYPES	91
4.4. CONVERTING COLUMNS	95
4.5. EXERCISE SECTION	99
4.5.1. EXERCISES	99
4.5.2. EXERCISE SOLUTIONS	100
5. CREATING AND MODIFYING TABLES	**101**
5.1. CREATING TABLES AND INSERT INFORMATION	101

5.2.	DELETING DATA AND DROPPING TABLES	**112**
5.3.	DELETING COLUMNS AND ALTERING TABLES	**116**
5.4.	EXERCISE SECTION	**121**
5.4.1.	EXERCISES	121
5.4.2.	EXERCISE SOLUTIONS	122

6. COMBINING TABLES — 123

6.1.	**INNER JOIN**	**123**
6.3	**MULTI-KEY JOINS**	**135**
6.4	**UNION OPERATIONS**	**142**
6.5	**EXERCISE SECTION**	**147**
6.5.1	EXERCISES	149
6.5.2	EXERCISE SOLUTIONS	150

7. MORE ON SELECT STATEMENTS — 151

7.1.	**SUBQUERIES**	**152**
7.2	**SELECT + INSERT INTO**	**157**
7.3	**EXERCISE SECTION**	**161**
7.3.1	EXERCISES	162
7.3.2	EXERCISE SOLUTIONS	163

8 UPDATING INFORMATION — 164

8.1	**UPDATE – SET – WHERE**	**164**
8.2	**EXERCISES**	**169**
8.2.1	EXERCISE	170
8.2.2	EXERCISE SOLUTIONS	170

9 ADVANCED FILTERING — 171

9.1	**THE NOT OPERATOR**	**171**
9.2	**ORDER OF OPERATIONS**	**174**
9.3	**WILDCARDS**	**177**

9.3.1	EXERCISE	181
9.3.2	EXERCISE SOLUTIONS	181

10 CONCLUSION 183

ABOUT THE AUTHOR 184

1. Introduction

Hello dear reader, and welcome to the world of Structured Query Language, or SQL!

SQL, better known as Structured Query Language, stands as one of the most widely used programming languages globally. Originating in 1974, SQL is tailored for querying data in relational databases and finds application across diverse industries, both in large corporations and smaller enterprises. And what makes SQL ubiquitous? Two essential features contribute to its widespread adoption:

- Flexibility: SQL integrates with contemporary programming languages like Python, R, and Java.
- Versatility in Job Roles: SQL caters to a multitude of professionals. Whether you're an Application Developer, IT Manager, Data Scientist, Data Analyst, or Cloud Engineer, SQL becomes an indispensable tool for tasks ranging from building and extracting to analysing and integrating data. Financial Analysts leverage it to extract data from financial statements, Data Engineers use it to consolidate diverse data sources, Data Scientists prepare data for machine learning models[1], and Marketing Analysts delve into historical trends and scrutinize A/B test results.

The comprehensive list of roles using SQL highlights its applicability to a variety of tasks, from basic queries to complex data manipulations. Regarding my background as data analyst and scientist, this realization struck me during my tenure at major corporations, witnessing the improved efficiency of analysts who added SQL to their skillset. **Relying solely on spreadsheet software to analyse data posed limitations, and SQL emerged as a game-changer.**

But beyond its practicality and versatility, there are other compelling reasons to delve into the SQL language:

- **Demand**: SQL skills are highly sought after in the market, positioning you as a valuable asset in the workforce.
- **Ease of Learning**: Compared to many other programming languages, SQL is user-friendly, featuring straightforward syntax and a near-conversational tone.

---

[1] Models used in the Artificial Intelligence field

- **Versatility with Data**: SQL empowers you to perform a wide range of tasks, from database setup and alterations to data extraction, manipulation, and analysis.

While mastering SQL may seem reserved for tech wizards, I assure you it's accessible to anyone with the right foundation. This conviction led to the creation of *SQL for Absolute Beginners* and this book provides an instructional approach tailored for newcomers, requiring only a fundamental comfort level with computer usage—**no prior programming knowledge will be assumed throughout these pages.**

Whether you're a student seeking guidance or a seasoned professional aiming to expand your horizons, I trust this book will fulfil your aspirations and arm you with the insights needed to grasp SQL Given that, what will we learn? Mainly, we will delve into the core features of the language, which include:

- Setting up and altering databases;
- Fetching, manipulating, and examining data within tables;
- Merging data from two or more distinct tables;
- Understanding the range of data types in SQL, a fundamental concept in database management;
- Adding data to tables.

Also, this book includes a variety of exercises designed to enhance your skills in SQL coding. And this is probably one of the most important sentences in this introduction: **I want to emphasize the importance of opening SQL while you skim through these pages. Coding along with the chapters and completing the exercises will greatly improve your skill.**

If you have an interest in working with data or databases, becoming proficient in SQL is a strategic decision that can yield long-term benefits, and I hope this book can contribute to your journey! A closing note: the foundation for this book is my Udemy course, "*SQL for Absolute Beginners*"[2]. While it's not essential, you're welcome to explore the video content by registering on the platform. Also, don't hesitate to reach out to me on LinkedIn[3]. I'd be thrilled to connect and assist you in your learning journey.

Thank you for buying this book and I'm extremely excited to be able to teach you SQL in the next pages. I honestly hope you find this book valuable in your journey. Let's start!

---

[2] https://www.udemy.com/course/sql-for-absolute-beginners/

[3] https://www.linkedin.com/in/ivobernardo/

2. Setting up MySQL

In this opening chapter, we'll install the software that will be integral to use throughout the book. A very important thing to know about the term "SQL" is that it typically refers to "Structured Query Language", a standardized framework for querying and managing databases. While SQL has a universal core, it has various implementations provided by multiple organizations, some of which are open-source[4] and have been integral to the tech industry for many years. For example, here are some standout SQL-based systems:

- PostgreSQL: Often called Postgres, it's a free, open-source relational database management system (RDBMS) known for its flexibility and adaptability. It's SQL-compliant, highly scalable, and a favorite for web, mobile, geospatial, and analytics applications.

- MSSQL: An abbreviation for Microsoft SQL Server, MSSQL is a widely-recognized enterprise-grade database system by Microsoft. It's designed to handle vast amounts of structured data and often pairs with other Microsoft offerings being used by thousands of companies around the world.

- MySQL: This renowned open-source RDBMS is celebrated for its user-friendliness, high performance, and versatile application compatibility. It supports a vast usage of applications and programming languages. In this book, we'll be using this one!

Don't worry, while there's a wide variety of SQL variants, it's worth noting that the foundational concepts are often transferable. **Even though some commands might be unique to a specific variant, mastering SQL in one environment will generally empower you to navigate others with ease.** In this book, I've chosen to focus on the MySQL implementation for primarily two reasons:

- MySQL Workbench[5] provides an intuitive user interface for crafting and executing queries.
- MySQL is open-source, meaning it's free to use. Thus, the only cost you've incurred to learn SQL is the purchase of this book!

---

[4] In open-source software, you have access to the entire source code of the software and you normally don't pay to use its main features.

[5] Workbench is the User Interface that we will use to code in SQL

Ivo Bernardo

Most database management systems[6] function as servers. In our setup, this server will operate silently in the background of your computer, aiding in the management and storage of data in a database format. You can interact with these servers either via the command line or through a graphical user interface[7], as we'll demonstrate. **While these servers can also be hosted remotely or in cloud environments, those details are beyond the scope of this book.**

In summary, throughout this book, we'll engage with *MySQL Server* and its accompanying tool, *MySQL Workbench*, which offers a user-friendly platform for interacting with our stored tables and databases.

---

[6] MySQL is a database management system that can store data in tables (row-column format).

[7] We will use MySQL Workbench for this one

2.1. Installing MySQL Server, Shell and Workbench

Setting up MySQL on your computer is straightforward. Although Oracle owns it, the Community Edition remains entirely free. This means you can establish a local server on your device without incurring any cost. Do note that the upcoming tutorial is related to Windows users. **For those using Mac or Linux, the installation process is a bit different since there isn't a combined package that installs both the MySQL Server and Workbench simultaneously.** While those users will still find this section beneficial, I'll also provide external links to guide Mac or Linux users through their respective installation processes.

With that said, let's get both programs up and running on our Windows computer. Begin by navigating to Google (**www.google.com**) and entering *"download mysql"* into the search bar, as depicted in figure 1.

Figure 1 – "download mysql" Google Search

Here, hit the first link on the page (or look for the link that redirects to the page https://www.mysql.com/downloads/. The link should take you to a page similar to the one shown in Figure 2.

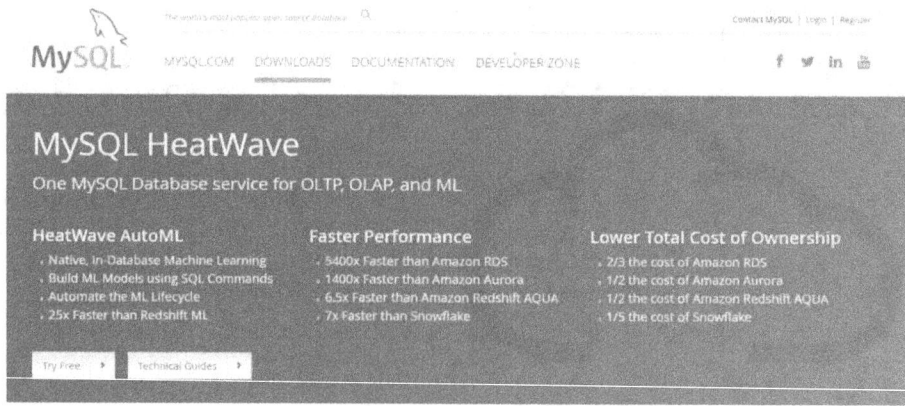

Figure 2 – MySQL Downloads Page

Keep in mind that the page on Figure 2 may have changed when you pick up this book. Nevertheless, it's expected that if you scroll until the end of the page, you'll see a link to **"MySQL Community (GPL) Downloads"**:

Figure 3 – MySQL Community (GPL) Downloads link

If for some reason the page changed completely, look for Community Downloads and you will be able to get to the MySQL download link. In the page we are seeing in Figure 3, hit the link *"My SQL Community (GPL) Downloads"* and you'll be taken to the page on Figure 4.

MySQL Community Downloads

- MySQL Yum Repository
- MySQL APT Repository
- MySQL SUSE Repository

- MySQL Community Server
- MySQL Cluster
- MySQL Router
- MySQL Shell
- MySQL Operator
- MySQL NDB Operator
- MySQL Workbench

- MySQL Installer for Windows

- C API (libmysqlclient)
- Connector/C++
- Connector/J
- Connector/NET
- Connector/Node.js
- Connector/ODBC
- Connector/Python
- MySQL Native Driver for PHP

- MySQL Benchmark Tool
- Time zone description tables
- Download Archives

Figure 4 – MySQL Community Downloads

I'm on a Windows computer, so I'll download the *MySQL Installer for Windows*:

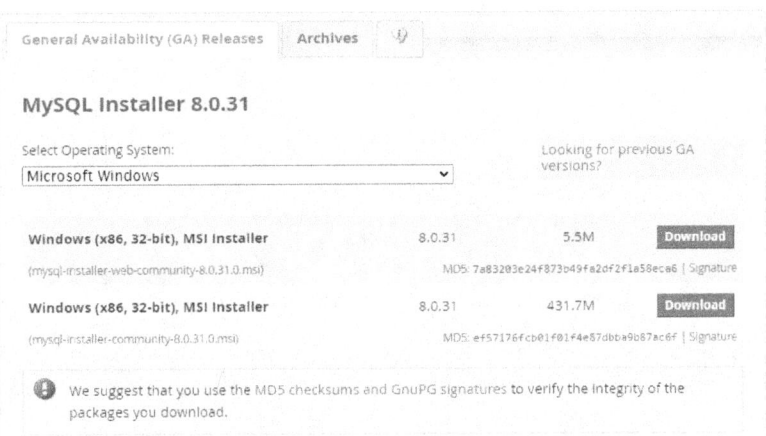

Figure 5 – MySQL Installer for Windows

At the time of my writing, the available version of MySQL is *8.0.31*.

If you have an Ubuntu operating system, please follow this link: **https://www.digitalocean.com/community/tutorials/how-to-install-mysql-on-ubuntu-20-04**.

If you have a Mac, you can find more instructions here **https://www.geeksforgeeks.org/how-to-install-mysql-on-macos/** and pick up MySQL Workbench here (**https://dev.mysql.com/downloads/workbench/**).

As mentioned, the primary distinction between the installation processes for Ubuntu and Mac is the absence of a unified installer that installs both MySQL Server and Workbench at once. In contrast, the Windows installer enables a quick installation of both components in one go. Returning to the Page on Figure 5, click on the '*Download*' button for the 431.7 MB file (listed as the second option in the image) – this will redirect you to Oracle's login page.

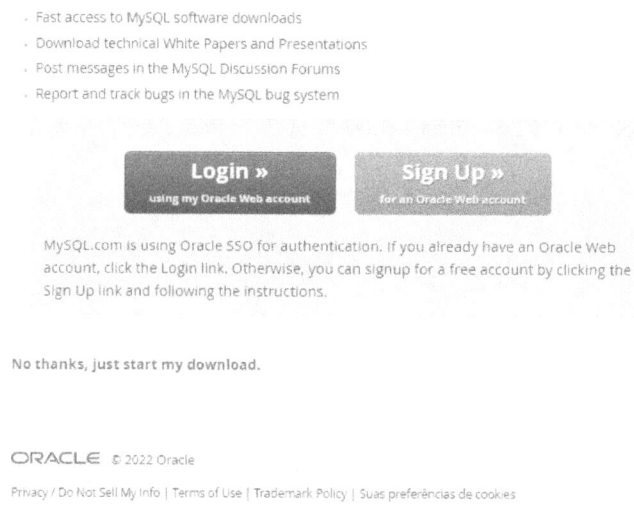

Figure 6 – MySQL Installer for Windows

Scroll all the way to the bottom of the page shown in Figure 6 and click on "*No thanks, just start my download.*" This action will initiate a download in your browser. Once the download is complete, you should see an icon that looks like the one on Figure 7 (or a similar one, depending on the software version you've downloaded) in your main downloads folder.

mysql-installer-c
ommunity-8.0.31
.0.msi

Figure 7 – MySQL Download File.

You can click on the install icon and this will launch a typical Windows install process:

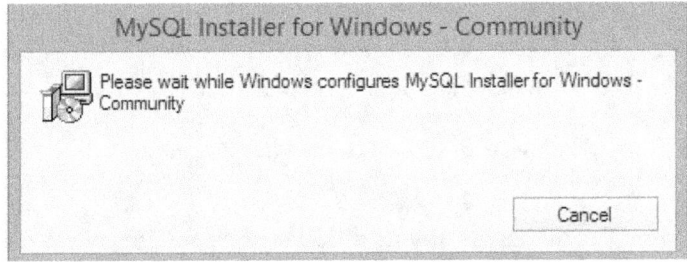

Figure 8 – MySQL Installer Process

This action will launch the MySQL installer, a utility designed to facilitate the installation of essential MySQL components. In the subsequent installation menu, select *"Developer Default"* to obtain the fundamental tools required to start working with and learning SQL queries. Primarily, our focus is on installing two main components: the **MySQL Server** (which hosts our local MySQL instance[8]) and the **MySQL Workbench** (our chosen user interface).

---

[8] The database server running on the background of our computer

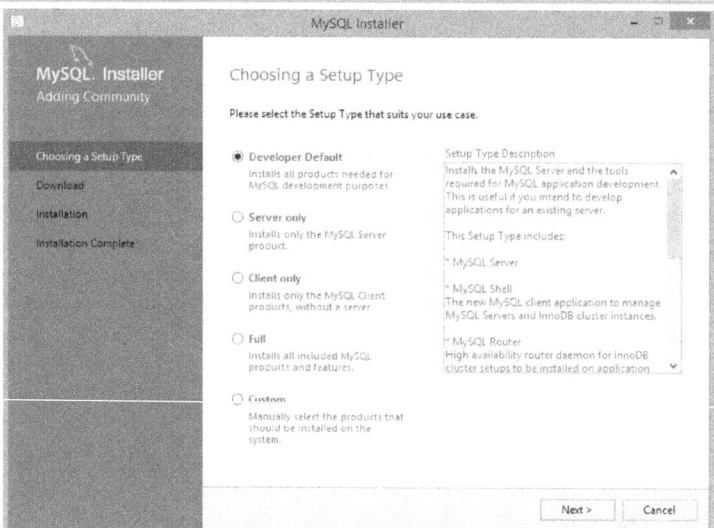

Figure 9 – MySQL Installer Window

After clicking "*Next*", MySQL will assess any additional prerequisites needed to install the required services. If you don't see any missing components related to "*MySQL Workbench*" or "*MySQL Server*", you can proceed by clicking "*Next*".

On my computer, as illustrated in Figure 10, there's one prerequisite I'm missing for "*MySQL for Visual Studio 1.2.10.*" However, because that particular product isn't relevant to this book, I'm choosing to proceed without installing it. If you encounter a similar situation, feel free to click "*Next*" without adding the required software, provided the missing components aren't requisites for "*MySQL Workbench*" or "*MySQL Server*".

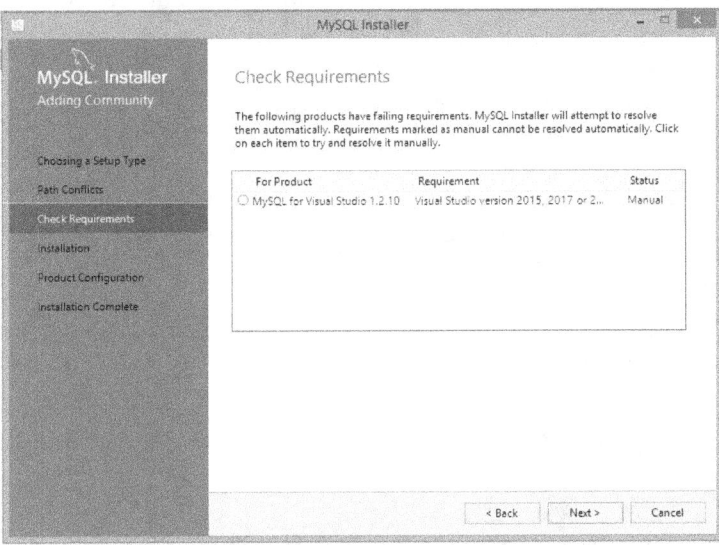

Figure 10 – Check Requirements Page

After navigating to the next page, MySQL will begin installing the necessary components on your system, as shown in Figure 11.

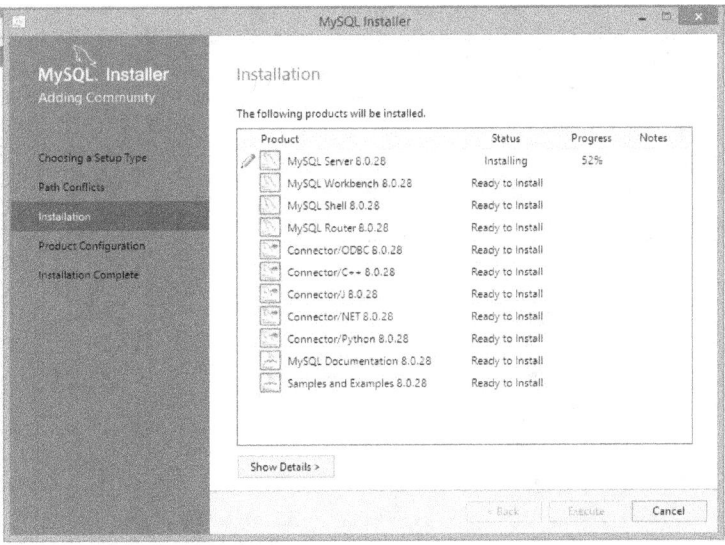

Figure 11 – MySQL Products Installation Page

In a few minutes, all the checks will turn green, indicating that the software was successfully installed on your computer:

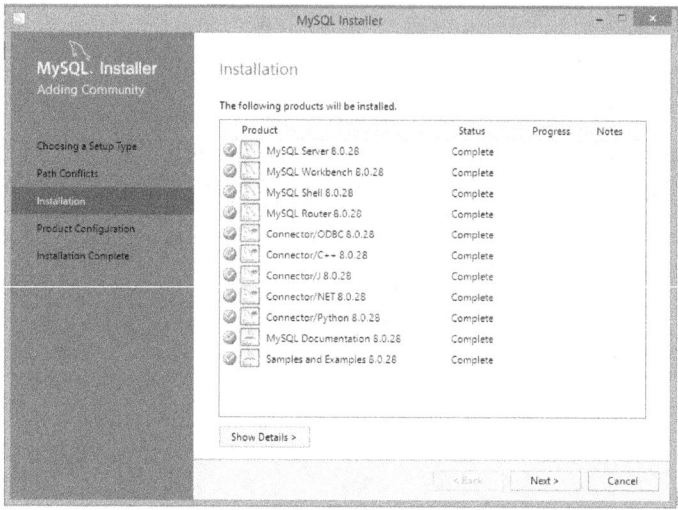

Figure 12 – MySQL Products Installation Page – Success

Click 'Next', and you'll be taken to the configuration window similar to the one on Figure 13.

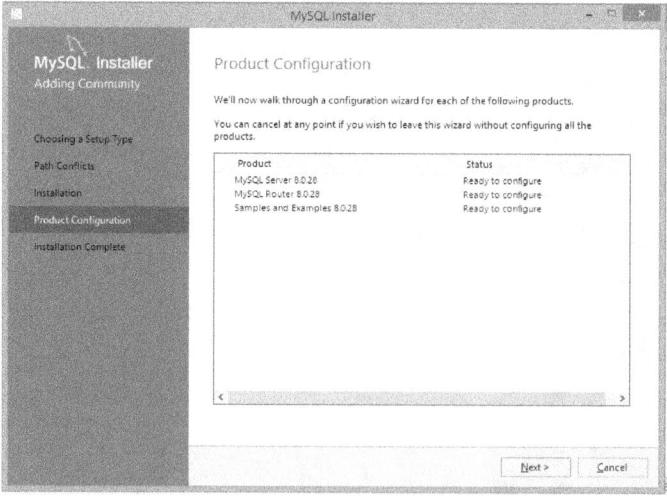

Figure 13 – Product Configuration Page

Hit "Next", again. In the *Type and Networking* window, leave everything as-is and hit next:

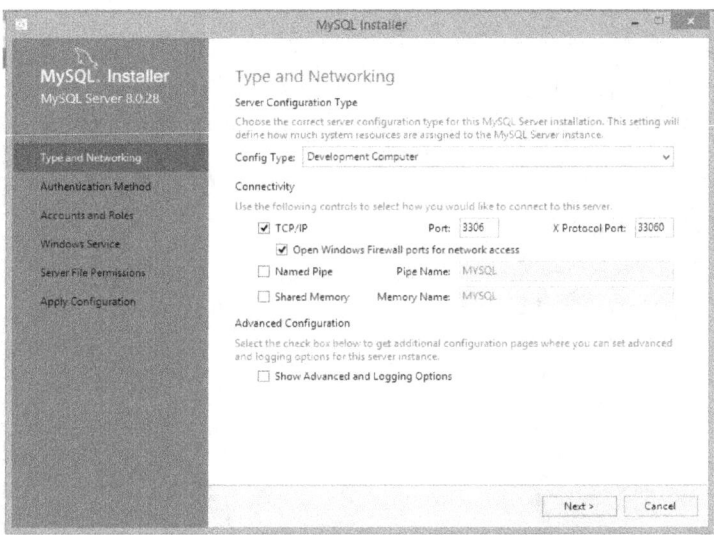

Figure 13 – Type and Networking Page

You will be taken to the configuration of the root user for MySQL server:

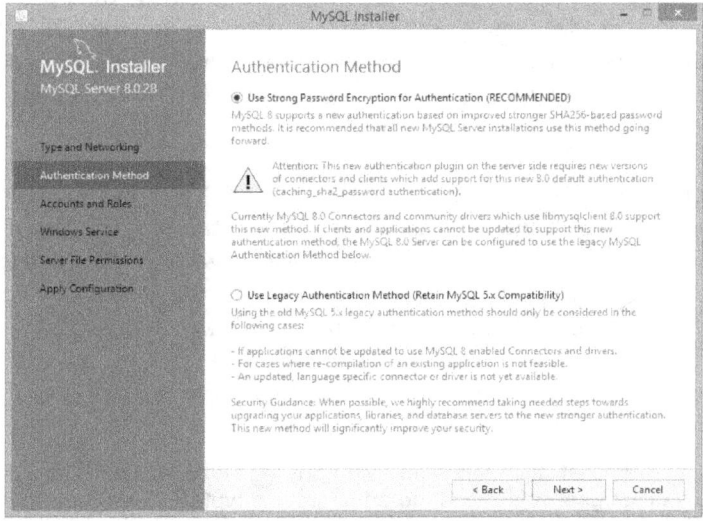

Figure 14 – Authentication Method Page

Choose "Use Strong Password" and go to the next page:

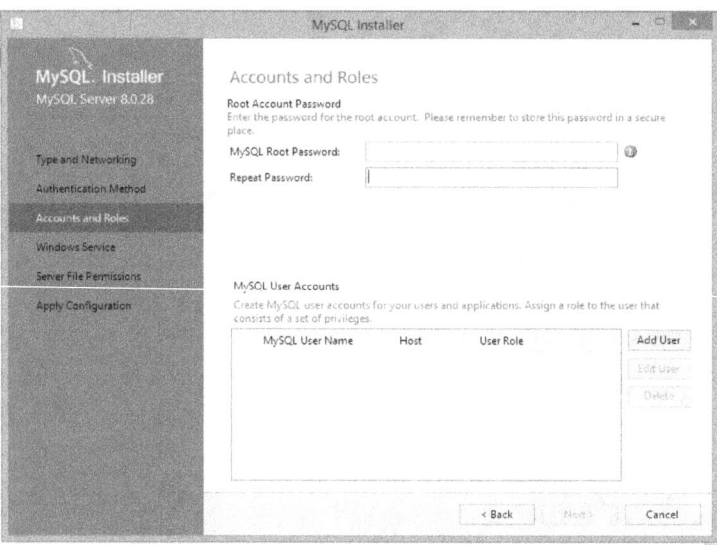

Figure 15 – Accounts and Roles

In this section, you'll be prompted to set a Root[9] password. Enter your desired password into the two fields labeled 'Root Account Password'. This establishes the password for the root (administrator) user – the credentials you'll use to connect to the SQL Server via MySQL Workbench. **It's crucial to record this password securely; you'll need it every time you interact with MySQL.** Ensure that the inputs for 'MySQL Root Password' and 'Repeat Password' match, as this is necessary to proceed with the installation.

In the window depicted in Figure 15, there's also an 'Add User' button, allowing you to create additional users. This step is optional at this point and we can skip it. Essentially, this process is configuring the user access to the MySQL Server, the software component that empowers your computer to process SQL commands. The *admin* user has the privileges to create, delete, and modify tables, which we'll cover in detail throughout this book.

---

[9] The "Root" user is an administrative account with privileges to execute all tasks in SQL. In many organizations, there are various user roles, and the admin role is typically assigned to a designated individual. For your personal setup, you can act as the root user.

After entering the same password into both fields, click 'Next', and a new window will appear.

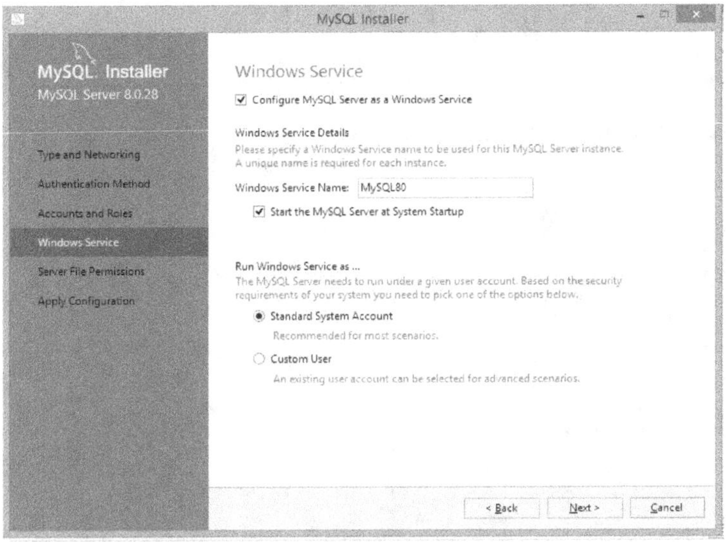

Figure 16 – Windows Service Page

You can stick with the default settings shown in Figure 16. However, if you prefer not to have the Server start when Windows boots up, deselect the "*Start the MySQL Server at System Startup*" option. If you do this, you'll need to manually start the server each time you boot your computer and wish to run queries on your MySQL data (we'll cover how to do this shortly).

If you leave the option selected, the server will automatically launch in the background when you start your computer. Once you've made your decision, click '*Next*', and you'll be presented with a window resembling Figure 17.

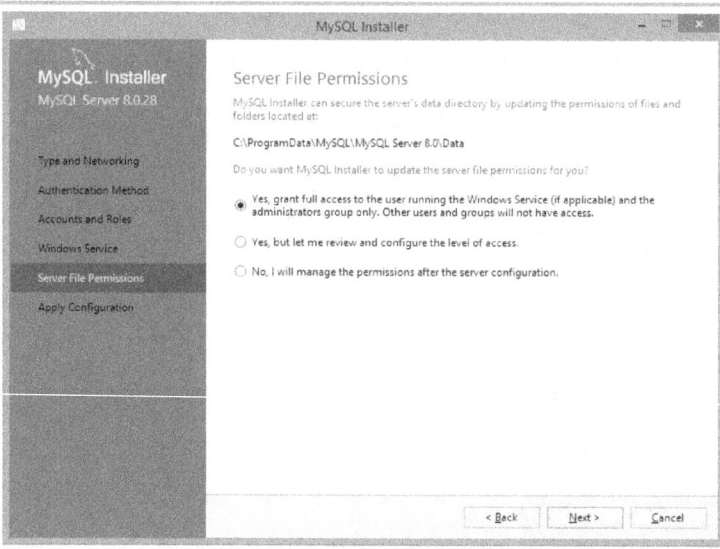

Figure 17 – Server File Permissions Page

Leave the default option and hit next.

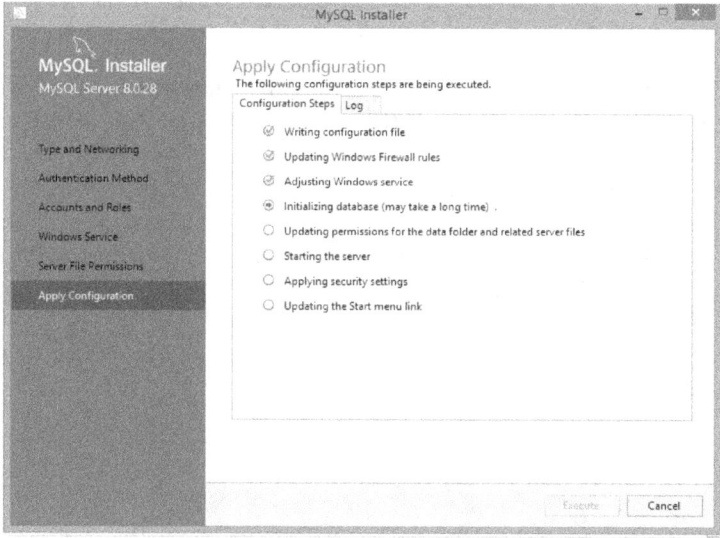

Figure 18 – Apply Configuration Page

Click '*Execute*' and allow the MySQL Installer to complete its final tasks. Once the process is done, click '*Finish*'.

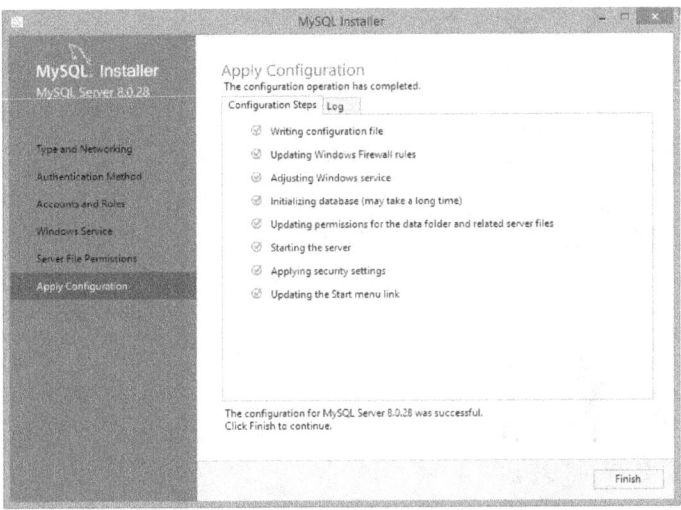

Figure 19 – Apply Configuration Page

If there are any additional products needing configuration, MySQL will prompt you after you click '*Finish*'. Proceed by clicking '*Next*'. For me, this leads to the MySQL Router Configuration.

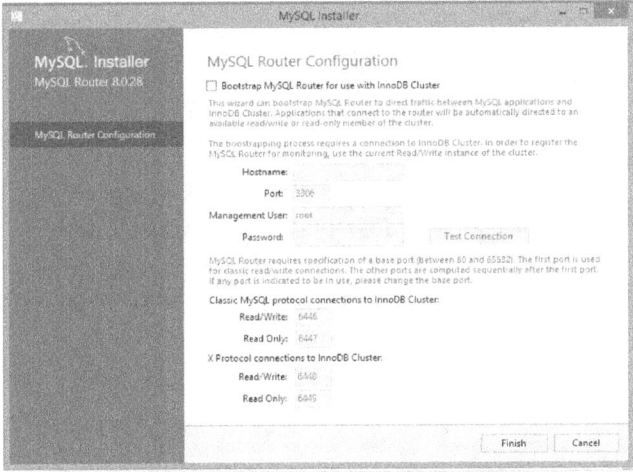

Figure 20 – MySQL Router Configurations

If this screen appears, click '*Finish*' with the default settings. On the following page, we'll begin the MySQL Server configuration, as depicted in Figure 21.

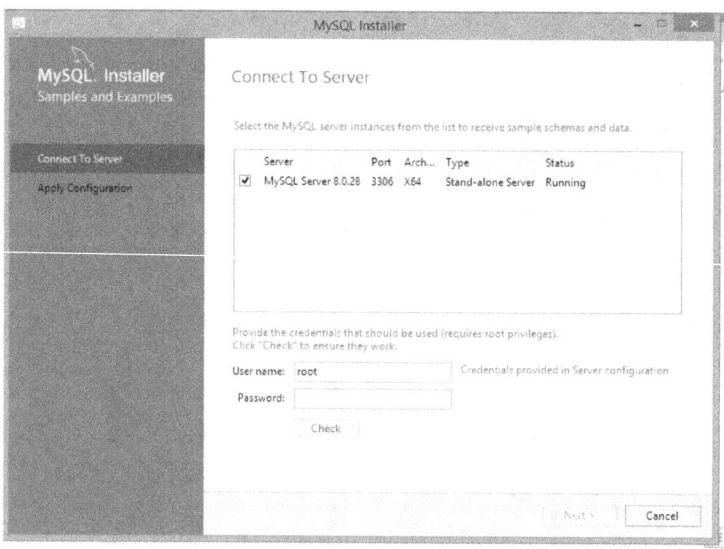

Figure 21 – MySQL Server Configuration

Write the root password you've defined before in the "Password" field and hit "Check":

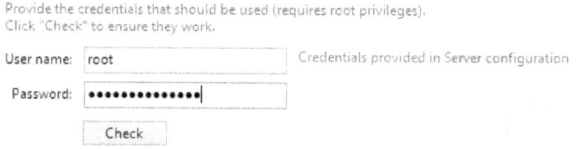

Figure 22 – MySQL Server Password Check

After hitting check, you should see a Success message similar to the one we are seeing on Figure 23.

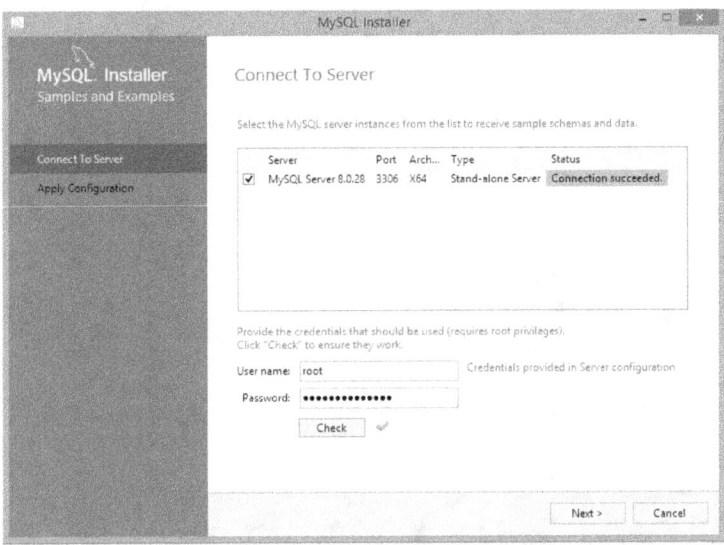

Figure 23 – Connect to Server Page

Hit "Next" to go the Server Configuration Page:

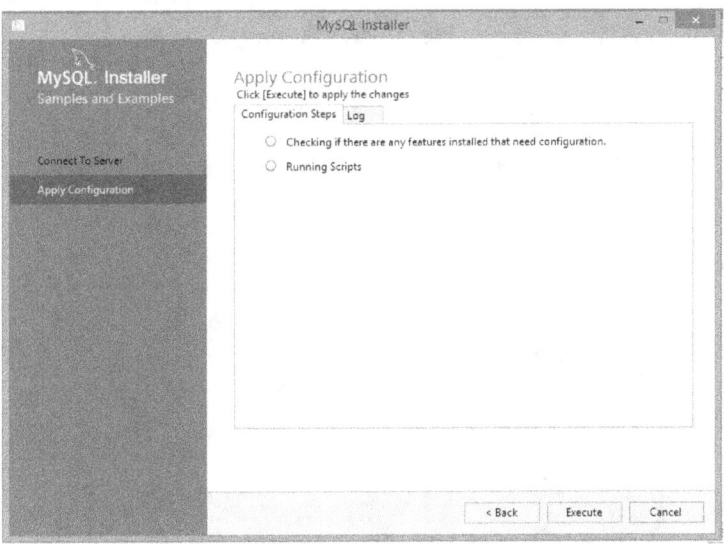

Figure 24 – Apply Configuration Page

On Figure 24, hit Execute to perform the required configurations on the server. If all checks show up, you can hit "Finish":

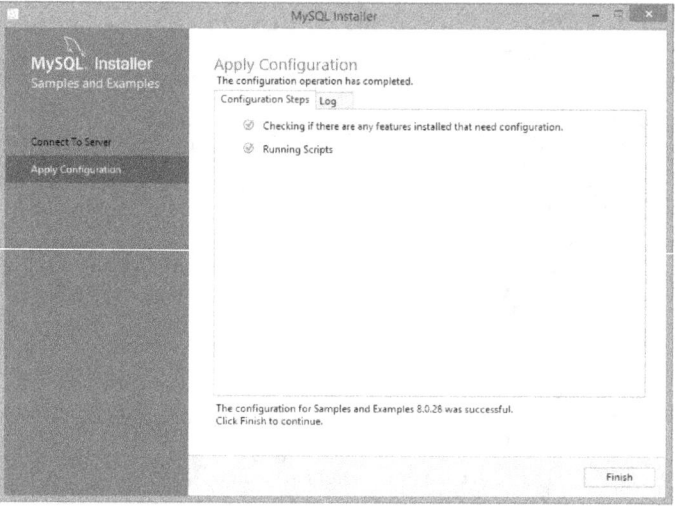

Figure 25 – Apply Configuration Page – Success Message

After the configuration ends, you can hit "Next" and "Finish":

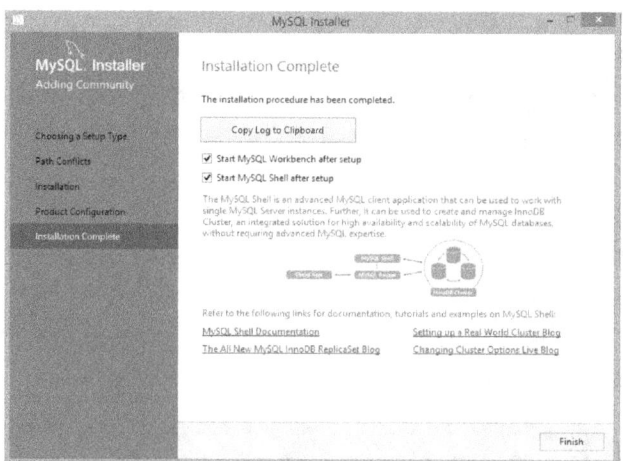

Figure 26 – Installation Complete Page

Following this, MySQL Workbench or a command line interface may pop up. For now, let's focus on MySQL Workbench, the main User Interface we will use throughout the book:

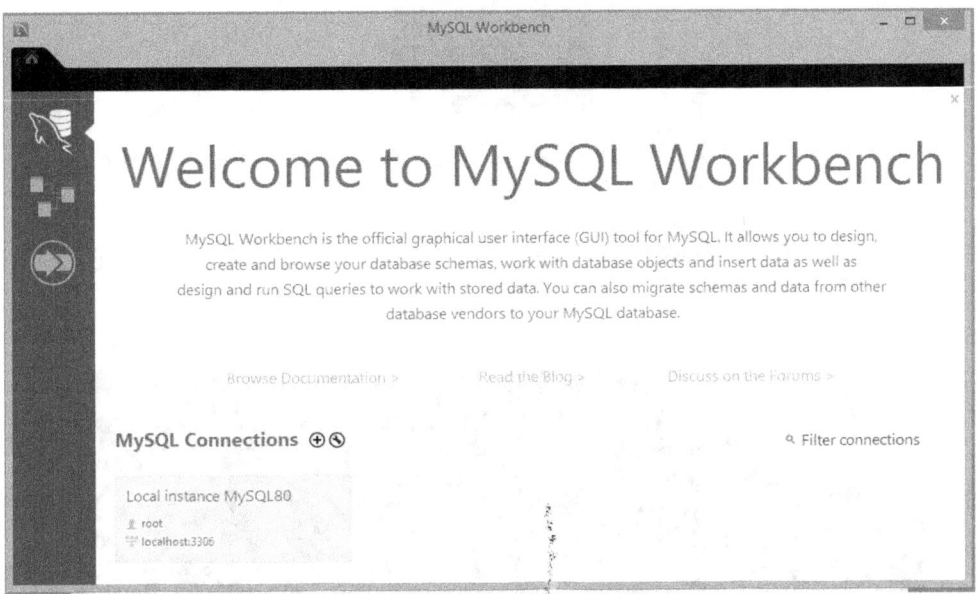

Figure 27 – MySQL Workbench

We'll be using this Graphical User Interface (GUI) throughout the book for writing our SQL code. MySQL Workbench offers a visual interface to access the database server running in the background of our computer. Much like after installing other software, you'll notice some new icons on your computer once you've set up MySQL. By using the Windows search bar and typing in '*MySQL*', you can see new software available for you:

Figure 28 – Windows Search Bar

Figure 29 – MySQL Workbench Icon

Other than "MySQL Workbench", you will also have "MySQL Shell" available:

Figure 30 – MySQL Shell

While we won't be using the command line interface for SQL coding in this book, it's worth opening the program to grasp its purpose. When you launch MySQL Shell, you'll be greeted with a command line interface.

Figure 31 – MySQL Shell Command Line Interface

This window can also be used to run the SQL commands we will learn throughout the book, although our preferred way will be using the Workbench interface. Also, as mentioned earlier in the chapter, the installation process for MySQL can be a bit more difficult for Mac or Ubuntu users. Specifically, you might need to install both the MySQL Server and Workbench as separate software packages. If you have one of those operating systems, I would recommend trying to find some tutorials on the Internet by searching for "MySQL Server install mac / ubuntu" or "MySQL Workbench mac / ubuntu". The links for installing Server and Workbench as standalone programs are here[10] and here[11].

---

[10] https://dev.mysql.com/downloads/mysql/

2.2. Launching MySQL Service from Scratch

If you opted out by unchecking the box labeled *"Start the MySQL Server at System Startup"* (as depicted in figure 16 of the previous chapter), then the upcoming section will be relevant to you. When the MySQL server initiates as you boot up Windows, it means that a local instance of the MySQL Server is immediately accessible every time you power on your computer. This enables you to fetch data right from the moment you boot your computer up, granting access to all tables that you have in the databases.

If not, we might need to manually activate MySQL Server. On Windows, this can be done by looking for *'Services'* using the Windows search tool:

Figure 32 – Services App in Windows

Double click the *"Services"* App and this will open a window similar to the one we see on Figure 33.

---

[11] https://dev.mysql.com/downloads/workbench/

Figure 33 –Windows Services

Scroll until you find the MySQL Service listed on your computer.

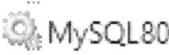

Figure 34 –MySQL Service

Locate the MySQL service, right-click on it, and select '*Start.*' After this action, you should notice the Status switch to **'Running'**:

Name	Description	Status
MySQL80		Running

Figure 35 –MySQL Service

When the MySQL service is active and 'Running', your server becomes accessible. **This allows you to create, query, or modify tables, which is vital for executing SQL queries on your computer (particularly the queries we will be going though in this book).** Only once you confirm that the Windows service is active should you proceed to open MySQL Workbench.

2.3. Getting familiar with MySQL Workbench

With our SQL server working on the background of our computer, it's time to get familiar with the User Interface we will use throughout the book to execute our SQL queries. If you search for "*MySQL Workbench*" in your operating system search tool[12], the following icon will pop up:

Figure 36 –MySQL Workbench Icon

Double click it and a window similar to the one on Figure 37 will open.

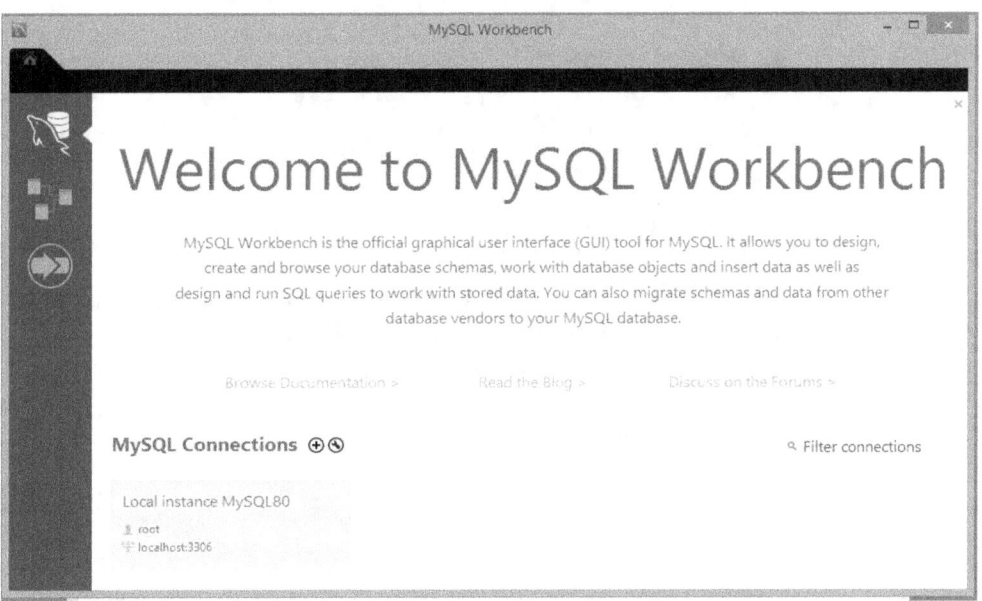

Figure 37 –MySQL Workbench Welcome window

---

[12] If you use Windows, you can use Windows Search

When you first open MySQL Workbench, you'll notice the homepage provides suggestions for servers you can connect to. If you've successfully installed MySQL Server, your *localhost* server should be displayed in the bottom-left corner of the window.

Figure 38 – Local Instance of MySQL Server

Let's click the box on Figure 38 as that will open a prompt that will let us type our server password:

Figure 39 – MySQL Server Password prompt

Type in the password you set during the installation. Once you've entered it, click on "*Ok*". In certain instances, this might lead you to a window resembling Figure 40.

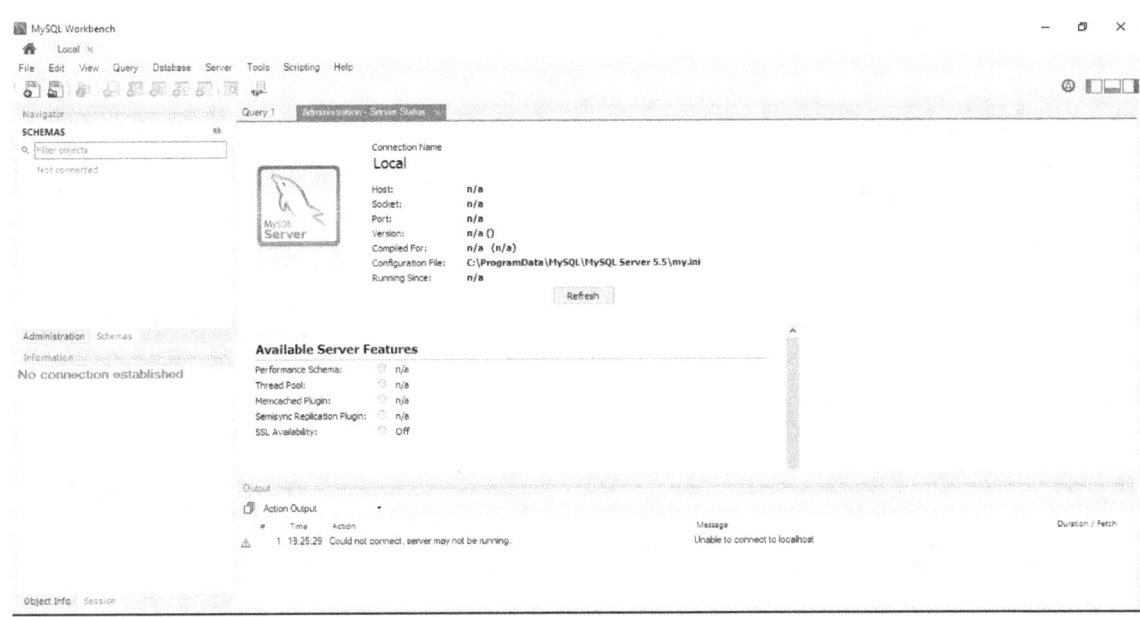

Figure 40 – MySQL Workbench "No Connection Established"

If you encounter this issue, it's because MySQL server is not running in the background and your user interface cannot communicate with it. Remember that Workbench is just an interface of MySQL that doesn't interpret the SQL code itself; the server must be active in your computer's background for the code to run.

If this occurs after entering your password, refer to Chapter 2.2 for steps on starting your server. After going through that process, relaunch MySQL Workbench.

If you now return to MySQL Workbench and try to connect to your server...

Figure 41 – MySQL WorkBench Home Page with Server Running

Voilá! Your MySQL server is up and running. The user interface might seem a bit complex at first glance, but I'll walk you through it since we'll be using it frequently in this book. Let's begin with the top navigation bar:

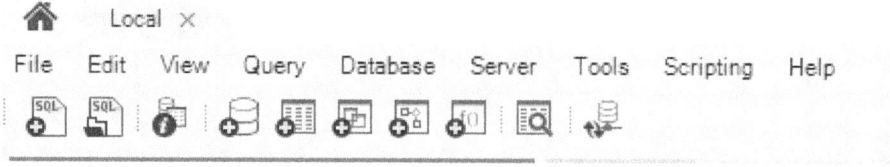

Figure 42 – MySQL Navigation Bar

In Figure 42, you'll find the menu that allows us to create new query files and explore specific features of MySQL Workbench. For instance, take a look at the *'Local'* tab at the top of the screen.

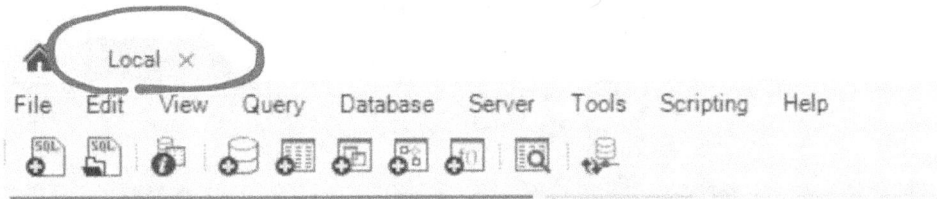

Figure 43 – MySQL Local Server Tab

The *'Local'* tab indicates that a connection to a local database server is active. If you've successfully connected to your MySQL server during the Workbench setup, this tab will be visible in your window. Directly beneath that, there's a versatile menu offering various functions. You can, for example, save query files, interact with the database server, or utilize a range of MySQL tools.

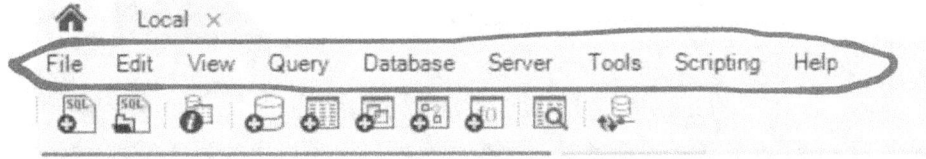

Figure 44 – MySQL Local Server Tab

Right below the navigation bar, we have quick access icons that we can use:

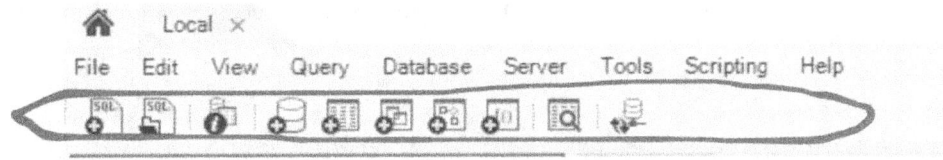

Figure 45 – Quick Navigation Bar

On the left side of the MySQL Workbench interface, you'll find the databases available for querying.

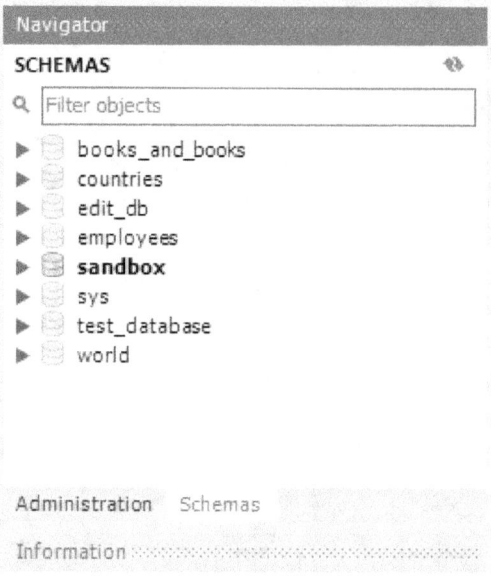

Figure 46 – Available Databases (Schemas)

These databases, often referred to as schemas in MySQL terminology, house tables and data that I can access using SQL code. Clicking on one of the arrows will expand the database, revealing more details about a specific schema. If you've just installed MySQL and find your environment empty or only containing the '*sys*' database, that's completely normal. We'll address that shortly!

Now, let's turn our attention to the most important window in the MySQL environment, the query window, shown on Figure 47.

Figure 47 – Query Window

We'll be writing our SQL code in this area throughout the book. At the top left corner of this window, you'll notice a tab labeled '*Query 1*'. This suggests we're working on a file named '*Query 1*' and typically, unsaved files are assigned these placeholder names, like '*Query 1*', '*Query 2*', and so forth.

Lastly, there's the 'Output' window situated beneath the query window, and it appears as follows:

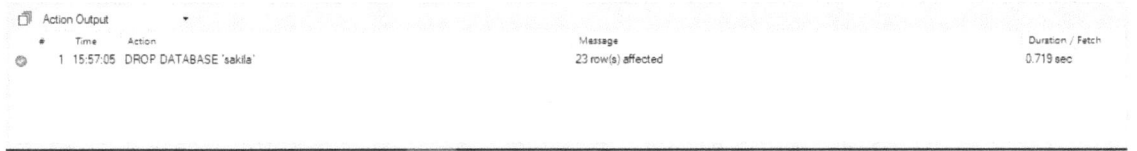

Figure 48 – Output Window

In your case, the window might be completely blank, signaling that no SQL commands have been executed. **In Figure 48, I've run an SQL command on my interface to give you a glimpse of what a successful SQL execution looks like.** In the *results* table, the first column displays an icon — either a checkmark or a cross. This signals whether the recent code execution was successful. However, don't stress about grasping every nuance of MySQL Workbench at this point, as we'll delve into these features in the upcoming sections. It's enough if you understand that MySQL Workbench offers an intuitive interface, allowing us to craft SQL code and engage directly with the databases hosted in our SQL server.

We're almost done setting up our learning environment! As highlighted before, you possible do not have a pre-existing database schema at your disposal to query. To ensure a productive learning curve, we'll address this by introducing a sample database named "*sakila*". This will give us the ability to practice and run our SQL commands on concrete data, making examples much easier to grasp. During the next section, I'll walk you through the steps of setting up the *sakila* database, one of the most famous "toy databases[13]" available for MySQL. After that, we'll start with the learning journey!

---

[13] A toy database is a database that contains fictional data used for educational purposes.

2.4. Setting up the Sakila Database

As mentioned before, during this book, we will use a database called *Sakila*[14]. The *sakila* database is a toy database that contains fictional information about movies, actors and other details regarding a fictional movie rental store (yes, if you are young, there was a business where you physically had to to rent movies, believe it or not!). This database is widely used as a practical example and it contains enough data for us to cover the use cases we'll need. To set it up, we will need to run 2 scripts that will do two different things:

- First, create the schema and structure of the tables.
- Then, we can use another script to populate the tables with data.

To start setting up the *sakila* database, head over to https://dev.mysql.com/doc/index-other.html and scroll down to the "Example Databases" section.

Example Databases

Title	DB Download	HTML Setup Guide	PDF Setup Guide
employee data (large dataset, includes data and test/verification suite)	GitHub	View	US Ltr | A4
world database	TGZ | Zip	View	US Ltr | A4
world_x database	TGZ | Zip	View	US Ltr | A4
sakila database	TGZ | Zip	View	US Ltr | A4
airportdb database (large dataset, intended for MySQL on OCI and HeatWave)	TGZ | Zip	View	US Ltr | A4
menagerie database	TGZ | Zip		

Figure 49 – Example Databases

In Figure 49, row number 4 contains the *sakila* database. You'll find a "*Zip*" link under the "*DB Download*" section. Clicking on this will initiate the download of a zip file similar to the one shown on figure 50:

Figure 50 – Sakila DB Zip File

---

[14] https://dev.mysql.com/doc/sakila/en/

Use a zip extraction tool, such as WinRar, WinZip, or 7Zip, to unpack the file on your computer. Once unzipped, you'll find a folder containing three files:

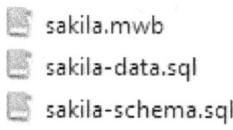

Figure 51 – Sakila DB Files

Double-click the '*sakila-schema.sql*' file, and it should prompt MySQL Workbench to open with the *sakila-schema* script loaded.

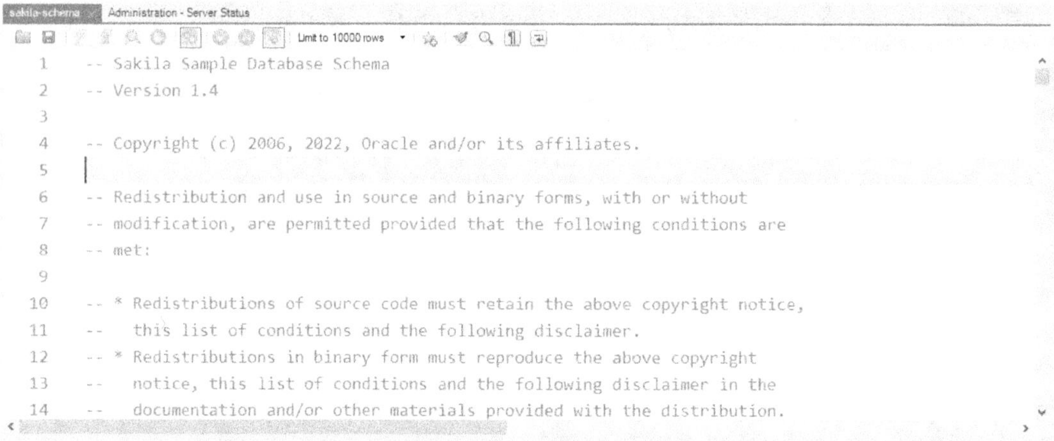

Figure 52 – Sakila Sample Database Schema File

What we've just done is open our first SQL file! This SQL file contains code that we can run in our server. And about the server, if yours isn't functioning properly, you'll see a message similar to the one on figure 53.

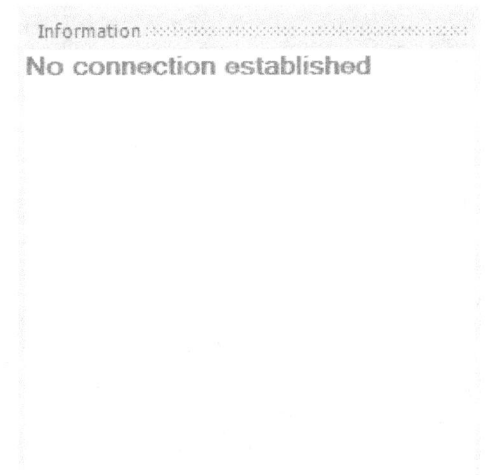

Figure 53 – No connection established – MySQL Workbench

If this happens, you need to connect to the localhost (server) manually. In the MySQL Workbench window, you can do this by clicking on the icon on Figure 54.

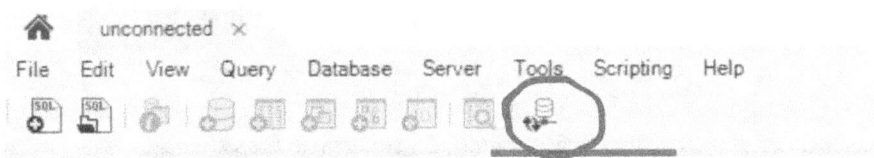

Figure 54 – MySQL Server Database Connection

After clicking the connection icon, MySQL might ask you for the root password. Once you enter it, you are logged on to the SQL server, and new information will show up in place of the "*No connection established*" notification.

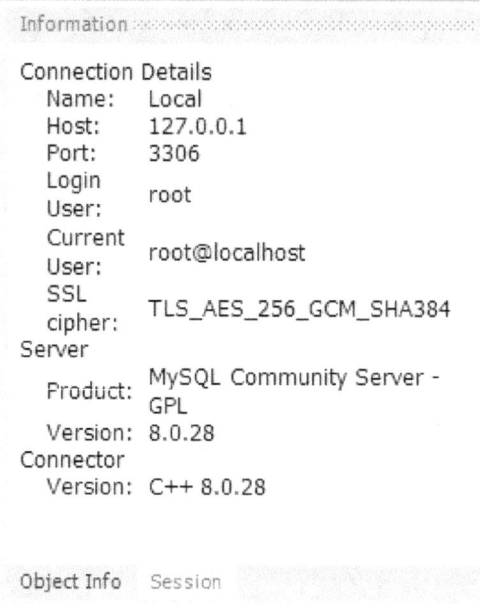

Figure 55 – MySQL Server Database Connection

Now that the server is connected, you can go back to the *sakila-schema.sql* script window. If MySQL has opened an **'Administration – Server Status'** tab, simply click on the '*sakila-schema*' tab right beside it, as shown in Figure 56.

Figure 56 – MySQL Workbench Tabs

Once on the *sakila-schema* tab, you will have the option to execute the current script. Executing SQL code in Workbench is a straightforward process and in the upcoming section, we will delve into executing statements with more comprehensive explanations. However, for now, it's important to note that you can execute the code by simply clicking on the lightning bolt icon, as illustrated in figure 57.

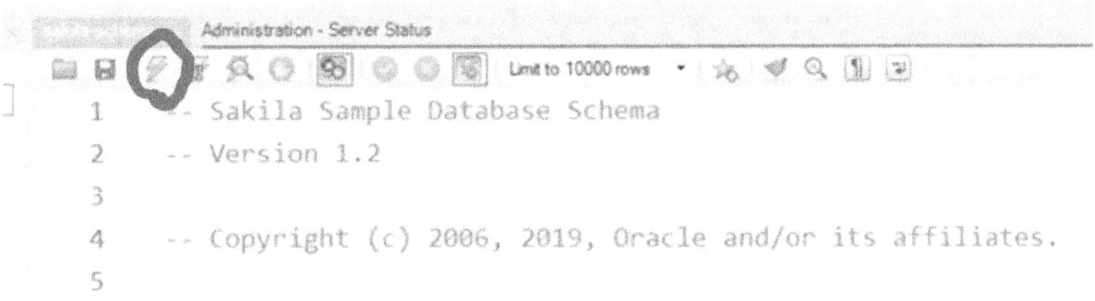

![Figure 57](mysql-workbench-execute.png)

Figure 57 – Executing SQL Code in MySQL Workbench

By clicking the highlighted button, you'll execute the entire code within this script. This SQL script is designed to establish the complete structure for the *sakila* database. While you may not be acquainted with the code just yet, don't worry – we'll delve into similar commands extensively throughout this book. For now, it's crucial that we can successfully create the table structure we'll be working with throughout the book.

Next, navigate to the '*refresh*' button near the schema list, located on the left side of MySQL Workbench.

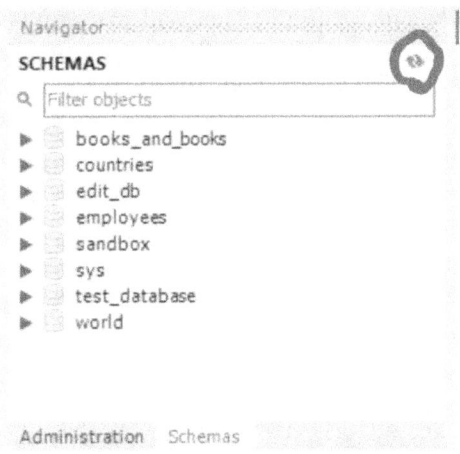

Figure 58 – Refresh Button on Schemas Navigator

.. after you click it, a new database will show up!

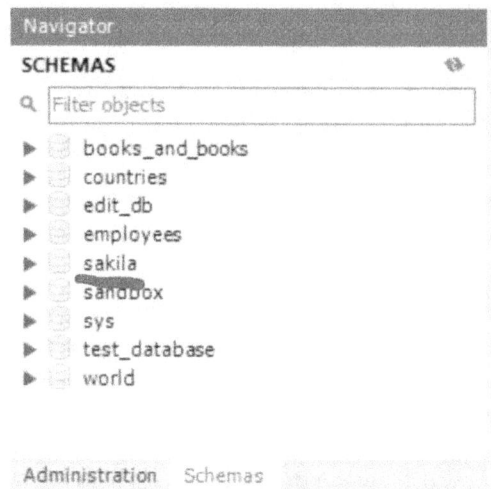

Figure 59 – List of Available Schemas in MySQL Workbench

If you see *sakila* here, we've successfully set up the *sakila* schema, creating all the crucial columns and rows for our fictional movie rental store. With this foundational structure ready, our next task is to fill it with pertinent data, truly enriching our database!

To do that, head up to the *sakila-data.sql* file, which will present yet another SQL script. This one will assist us in populating our tables with data, adding information about movies, actors and other details. Open the script in SQL, just like we've done with the *sakila-schema.sql* file.

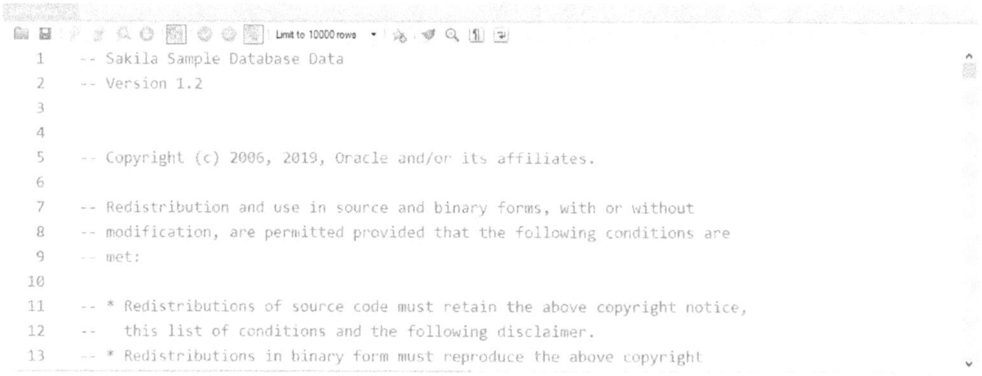

Figure 60 – sakila-data.sql file

If you check closely the *'run'* icon (depicted as a thunderbolt) is dimmed upon opening the new file and this might indicate a need to reconnect to the server. To correct that situation, simply click on the *'connect'* icon to link the script back to the server. Once connected, use the *'run'* icon to populate the *sakila* database by executing the entire *sakila-data.sql* file, similarly to how we've executed the *sakila-schema.sql*.

If you're experiencing difficulties executing the *sakila-data.sql* file, just return to the steps we took with the *sakila-schema*, but apply them to the *sakila-data* file. The good part is that after successfully executing the *sakila-data.sql* file, you should be all set to dive into the book! And how can we verify that the *sakila* database has been set up correctly? First, after you've executed the *sakila-data.sql* script, start a fresh, blank file within MySQL Workbench by clicking the highlighted icon in Figure 61.

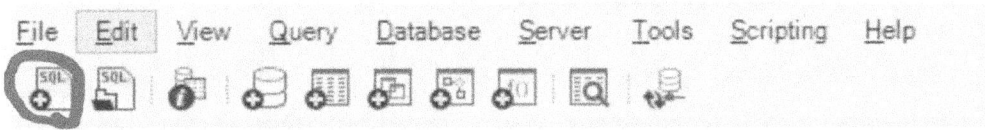

Figure 61 – New SQL File Icon

As soon as you click this icon, you open a new blank SQL script in Workbench:

Figure 62 – Blank SQL Script in MySQL WorkBench

We'll use this new script file[15] to verify the proper setup of our *sakila* database, and it'll also serve as our first attempt at crafting SQL code from the ground up.

---

[15] A "script" is a name typically given to a set of coding instructions.

In the provided window, write down the following code. If this seems cryptic now, don't worry; we'll delve into its details in the upcoming chapter.

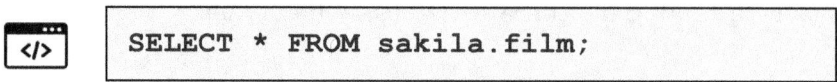

```
SELECT * FROM sakila.film;
```

A small note: this is the first time we are using a **code block** in the book. Every time you see this icon , that's the cue to open MySQL workbench and start coding! Next to every icon we will have a SQL instruction for us to write. So, whenever you come across a code block, hop over to the MySQL Workbench query window and input the given code, as shown in Figure 63:

Figure 63 – Writing SQL Code in the MySQL Window

Looking at the code sitting near  and writing it in a SQL file will be the main way you can use to follow the instructions on this book. Should you need to run particular statements (given that SQL Workbench enables simultaneous execution of multiple instructions), simply highlight the desired code with your mouse, as demonstrated in Figure 64.

Figure 64 – Highlighting SQL Code in the MySQL script

After highlighting the code, click on the lightning bolt icon or press *CTRL + Enter*. This will run the code and display the results in an output window, similar to the one shown in Figure 65.

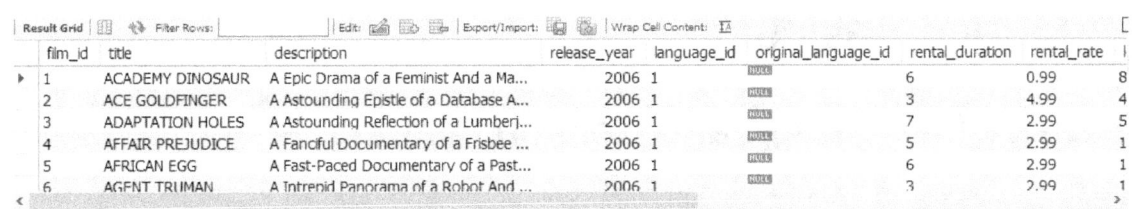

Figure 65 – SQL Output Window

Typically, when we draft a SQL statement, it results in a new output being generated, unless the statements are intended to change table structures. The outcome of SQL queries usually looks similar to what's illustrated in Figure 65. If you ran the command **SELECT * FROM sakila.film;** and saw an output table beneath the script window, it indicates you've successfully connected to the *sakila* database and you are ready to proceed with the book!

Remember, throughout the book we'll see code and output together – make sure you understand the connection between the two:

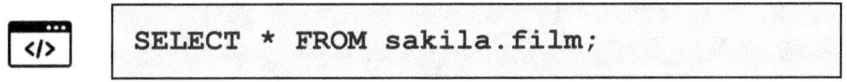

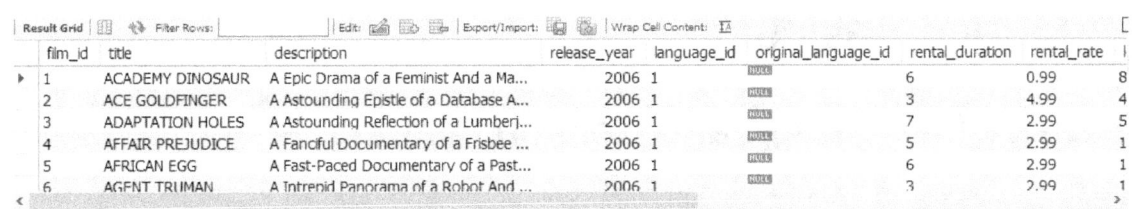

Figure 66 – SQL Output Window

Finally, we've finished the setup of MySQL! Taking the time to properly set up MySQL Workbench was essential since it lays the foundation for our coding journey. Now that we have everything ready, navigating through MySQL should be much smoother. If you encountered any hiccups while setting up the *sakila* database, check out this YouTube[16] video for an alternative walkthrough.

Let's start our coding journey!

---

[16] https://www.youtube.com/watch?v=bDKY_c4PRQA

3. Query Basics

3.1 Query Introduction and Column Filtering

In this section, we'll start by breaking down the core components of a SQL query. When we use the term "query," we're referring to a SQL statement that interacts with the data we have on our servers. **These statements play an essential role in fetching and modifying data within databases.**

Most data retrieval queries kick off with the **SELECT** keyword. For instance, if we wanted to pull all the data from the *'film'* table, we'd use a statement similar to the one we've seen in the last chapter:

```
SELECT * FROM sakila.film;
```

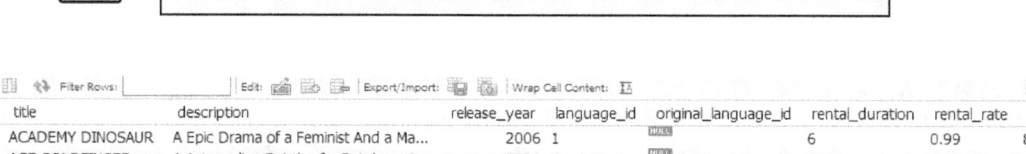

*Figure 67 – Preview of Output Query from "select * from sakila.film"*

Let's take it break down this query step-by-step:

- We begin with the **SELECT** keyword, signalling our intention to retrieve data from a table.

- The asterisk (*) indicates that we **want data from all columns within the table** (we'll delve deeper into this shortly).

- Next, with "**FROM sakila.film**", we specify to MySQL the exact table we're interested in. In MySQL, the common syntax for referencing tables is "*database_name.table_name*".

This is the simplest query example we can provide, which can be interpreted as: *'I want all columns and all rows from the sakila.film table.'* Moving forward, I'll also reference an accompanying image to aid in translating SQL code into plain English:

"I want all columns and all rows from the sakila.film table"

To help you better navigate the transition between conversational English and SQL code, I'll place a conversation icon[17] next to most SQL segments. This will help you switch between everyday English and SQL syntax—a critical skill when working with database queries and that should help you making the logical jump between natural and querying language.

As mentioned, we've used the asterisk to select all columns from the table, but what if we only want a few columns in our result? Say, we're interested in just the movie title and its release year? We can achieve this by simply swapping out the asterisk with the desired column names, separated by a comma:

```
SELECT title, release_year
FROM sakila.film;
```

title	release_year
ACADEMY DINOSAUR	2006
ACE GOLDFINGER	2006
ADAPTATION HOLES	2006
AFFAIR PREJUDICE	2006
AFRICAN EGG	2006
AGENT TRUMAN	2006

Figure 68 – Preview of Output Query from Column Subset Query

Now, we are asking SQL to retrieve the following:

"I want all rows but only the title and release_year columns from the sakila.film table"

---

[17] Icon attribution to https://www.flaticon.com/authors/freepik

When we swap the * for **'title'** and **'release_year'**, we're instructing SQL to retrieve only those two columns from the table. As a result, our output will now display a select subset of columns.

Moving on to another common practice in basic **SELECT** statements is using aliases. Let's say we want the **'release_year'** column to appear with the name **'Year'** and **'title'** to display as **'Movie Title'**:

```
SELECT title as movie_title, release_year as year
FROM sakila.film;
```

movie_title	year
ACADEMY DINOSAUR	2006
ACE GOLDFINGER	2006
ADAPTATION HOLES	2006
AFFAIR PREJUDICE	2006
AFRICAN EGG	2006
AGENT TRUMAN	2006

Figure 69 – Preview of Output Query from Aliases Example

In conversational English, we are asking for:

"I'd like to retrieve all rows, but only the 'title' and 'release_year' columns from the sakila.film table. Moreover, 'release_year' should be displayed as 'Year', and 'title' should show up as 'Movie Title'."

It's important to note that this command doesn't change the actual table. Instead, it only changes the column names displayed in our query's results. In the actual table, the columns remain labeled as **'title'** and **'release_year'**. **The nuances of this will become more evident as we delve into scripts that modify our tables later in the book.**

Essentially, what we've done is assigned an alias to our column names. The mechanics of using aliases for column names are straightforward:

- *original_column_name* as *new_column_name*

The `'as'` keyword allows us to rename columns in our output on the fly. But, we can also apply aliases to tables and then utilize those aliases when selecting columns – for example:

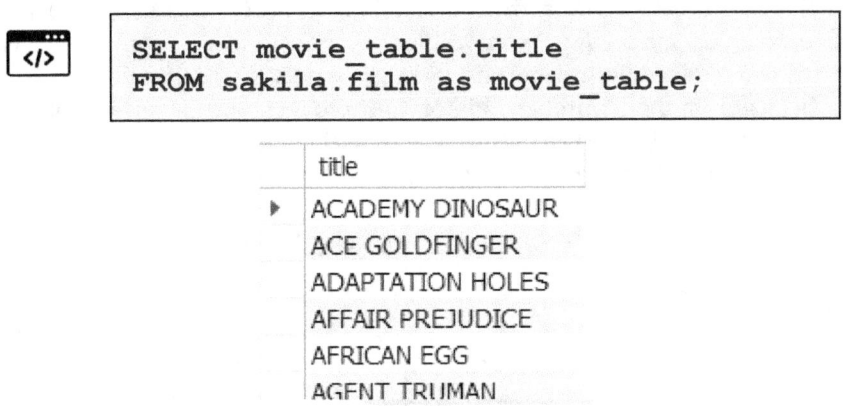

Figure 70 – Preview of Output Query from Table Alias Example

In the given code, we've designated the *'sakila.film'* table as *'movie_table'*. Consequently, if we want to reference column names from the table, we need to use the alias in the following format: *movie_table.column_name*. Notice that the query using the aliases behaves exactly the same as the following query:

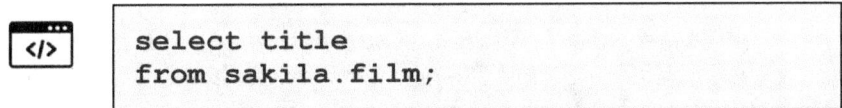

While the benefit of aliases might not be immediately obvious in this simple example, they prove invaluable when dealing with multiple tables in a single query. Aliases not only allow us to distinguish between columns from different tables but also enhance the clarity and readability of our code.

Now that we have an understanding of how aliases work, let's explore their application in conjunction with one of the most important SQL clauses – the **WHERE** clause. Having touched upon the basics of column filtering, you might be wondering: can we apply similar filters to our rows and only subset a specific portion of them? Absolutely! To do this, we'll delve into the details of the **WHERE** clause.

3.2 Where Statements

When working with SQL, filtering data from tables is a common and essential task. Often, users employ SQL to extract specific rows from tables. For instance, a common scenario involves retrieving rows from a table where a certain column meets a specific condition. This could be filtering customers based on their purchase history, employees with a certain job title, or products within a particular price range. The flexibility of SQL's filtering capabilities ensures that users can tailor their queries to extract the exact information they need.

To achieve these goals, one simply introduces a new clause: the **WHERE** statement.

```
select *
from sakila.film
where title = 'BULL SHAWSHANK';
```

film_id	title	description	release_year	language_id	original_language_id
105	BULL SHAWSHANK	A Fanciful Drama of a Moose And a S...	2006	1	NULL
NULL	NULL	NULL	NULL	NULL	NULL

Figure 71 – Preview of Output Query from WHERE clause example

Note: At times, I may opt to display only a subset of output columns in the figures throughout this book. For instance, while the table in Figure 71 showcases more columns in the actual output, some have been excluded in the screenshot to ensure clarity and readability.

In the mentioned query, we encounter a new piece of SQL syntax: **WHERE TITLE = 'BULL SHAWSHANK'**. This additional clause isolates movies in the table with the title **'BULL SHAWSHANK'** – in this way our output contains just one row as we only have one movie with this name. To put the query into simple conversational terms:

> I'd like to retrieve all columns but only those rows from the sakila.film table where the title matches 'BULL SHAWSHANK'.

The '=' symbol enables us to verify equality. On the opposite, for examinations of inequality, the '!=' symbol can be used:

```
select *
from sakila.film
where title != 'BULL SHAWSHANK';
```

film_id	title	description	release_year	language_id	original_language_id	rental_duration	rental_rate	leng
1	ACADEMY DINOSAUR	A Epic Drama of a Feminist And a Ma...	2006	1	NULL	6	0.99	86
2	ACE GOLDFINGER	A Astounding Epistle of a Database A...	2006	1	NULL	3	4.99	48
3	ADAPTATION HOLES	A Astounding Reflection of a Lumberj...	2006	1	NULL	7	2.99	50
4	AFFAIR PREJUDICE	A Fanciful Documentary of a Frisbee ...	2006	1	NULL	5	2.99	117
5	AFRICAN EGG	A Fast-Paced Documentary of a Past...	2006	1	NULL	6	2.99	130

Figure 72 – Preview of Output Query from inequality example

Note: To improve clarity, I might occasionally omit rows in the output illustrations, as demonstrated in Figure 72.

The given query retrieves all movies, except those with the title "BULL SHAWSHANK". Simply put, it means:

> "I want all columns but only the rows where title is not equal to BULL SHAWSHANK from the sakila.film table"

Another important point about the two previous queries is that **'BULL SHAWSHANK'** is wrapped in quotes. This happens because we're using a column full of regular text. In the upcoming section of this book, we'll discuss data types in greater depth but it's worth mentioning that filtering text isn't the same as filtering numbers or dates.

But before jumping into that, let's continue studying the **WHERE** clause. Imagine we would like to filter multiple movies at the same time – is this possible in SQL? Yes, as we have the option to use the **'IN'** clause.

```
select *
from sakila.film
where title IN ('BULL SHAWSHANK',
'AIRPORT POLLOCK');
```

film_id	title	description	release_year	language_id	original_language_id	rental_duration	rental_rate	length
8	AIRPORT POLLOCK	A Epic Tale of a Moose And a Girl who...	2006	1	NULL	6	4.99	54
105	BULL SHAWSHANK	A Fanciful Drama of a Moose And a S...	2006	1	NULL	6	0.99	125

Figure 73 – Preview of Output Query from multiple select example

In this last query, we are asking for the following:

I'd like to retrieve all columns from the 'sakila.film' table, but I'm only interested in rows where the title is either 'BULL SHAWSHANK' or 'AIRPORT POLLOCK'.

The `'IN'` function allows us to filter multiple titles simultaneously by enclosing them in parentheses. By separating each title with a comma, we can effectively select any combination of titles we're interested in.

The exact same output can be expressed using the `'OR'` query:

```
select *
from sakila.film
where title = 'BULL SHAWSHANK' OR
title = 'AIRPORT POLLOCK';
```

film_id	title	description	release_year	language_id	original_language_id	rental_duration	rental_rate	length
8	AIRPORT POLLOCK	A Epic Tale of a Moose And a Girl who...	2006	1	NULL	6	4.99	54
105	BULL SHAWSHANK	A Fanciful Drama of a Moose And a S...	2006	1	NULL	6	0.99	125

Figure 74 – Preview of Output Query from OR clause

One downside of using **OR** to filter data from a single column is that we end up repeating the 'column=value' pattern multiple times. For simplicity and efficiency, it's usually best to use the **IN** function when you're applying **OR** conditions to the same column.

However, don't write off the **OR** function just yet! It becomes particularly useful when setting conditions based on different columns. For example imagine we would like to retrieve the movie with title "Bull Shawshank" and all movies whose rental rate is less than 1.99:

```
select *
from sakila.film
where title = 'BULL SHAWSHANK' OR
rental_rate < 1.99;
```

film_id	title	description	release_year	language_id	original_language_id	rental_duration	rental_rate
1	ACADEMY DINOSAUR	A Epic Drama of a Feminist And a Ma...	2006	1	NULL	6	0.99
11	ALAMO VIDEOTAPE	A Boring Epistle of a Butler And a Cat ...	2006	1	NULL	6	0.99
12	ALASKA PHANTOM	A Fanciful Saga of a Hunter and a Pas...	2006	1	NULL	6	0.99
14	ALICE FANTASIA	A Emotional Drama of a A Shark And ...	2006	1	NULL	6	0.99
17	ALONE TRIP	A Fast-Paced Character Study of a C...	2006	1	NULL	3	0.99

Figure 75 – Preview of Output Query from OR clause

The query above translates into the following sentence:

I'd like to retrieve all columns from the sakila.film table, but I'm only interested in rows where the title is 'BULL SHAWSHANK' or the movie's rental rate is less than $1.99.

In this scenario, our search will display movies that meet one of the following criteria:

- The title is 'BULL SHAWSHANK.'
- The rental rate is less than $1.99.

With this query, if a movie appears in the results and its rental rate is $1.99 or more, then that movie must be 'BULL SHAWSHANK. However, it's probably more common that we want to filter only the movies that satisfy both criteria simultaneously. To do that, we can use the `'AND'` clause!

```
select *
from sakila.film
where title = 'BULL SHAWSHANK' AND
rental_rate < 1.99;
```

film_id	title	description	release_year	language_id	original_language_id	rental_duration	rental_rate	length
105	BULL SHAWSHANK	A Fanciful Drama of a Moose And a S...	2006	1	NULL	6	0.99	125
NULL	NULL	NULL	NULL NULL	NULL	NULL	NULL	NULL	NULL

Figure 76 – Preview of Output Query from AND clause

I'd like to retrieve every column from the sakila.film table, but only for those rows where the title is 'BULL SHAWSHANK' and the movie's rental rate is under $1.99.

Clearly, given that the title `'BULL SHAWSHANK'` is a required condition, only one movie will appear in the results as there's only one movie with that name. A more illustrative example of the **AND** clause in the *sakila* database is trying to retrieve all movies from 2006 with less than 1.99 of rental rate:

```
select *
from sakila.film
where release_year = 2006 AND
rental_rate < 1.99;
```

film_id	title	description	release_year	language_id	original_language_id	rental_duration	rental_rate
1	ACADEMY DINOSAUR	A Epic Drama of a Feminist And a Ma...	2006	1	NULL	6	0.99
11	ALAMO VIDEOTAPE	A Boring Epistle of a Butler And a Cat ...	2006	1	NULL	6	0.99
12	ALASKA PHANTOM	A Fanciful Saga of a Hunter And a Pas...	2006	1	NULL	6	0.99
14	ALICE FANTASIA	A Emotional Drama of a A Shark And ...	2006	1	NULL	6	0.99
17	ALONE TRIP	A Fast-Paced Character Study of a C...	2006	1	NULL	3	0.99

Figure 77 – Preview of Output Query from AND clause

In this scenario, we're choosing movies that meet two specific criteria:

- The movie was released in 2006.
- Its rental rate is less than $1.99.

Translating the sentence above into plain English:

I'd like to retrieve all columns from the sakila.film table, but only the rows where the movie was released in 2006 and has a rental price below $1.99.

In essence, using the **AND** clause ensures that all conditions within the **WHERE** clause are met in the results. Conversely, with the **OR** clause, a row only needs to satisfy one of the conditions to be included in the output.

Ok, cool. Now, it's time to introduce more comparison operators, that align pretty well with **WHERE** clauses. So far, we've discussed equality, inequality, and the less than symbol (<). Naturally, there are other standard comparison operators commonly found in mathematics that we are able to use in the language. For instance, to select all rows with values less than or equal to $0.99, you'd use the **<=** symbol:

```
select *
from sakila.film
where rental_rate <= 0.99;
```

This will output not only the rows with *rental_rate* less than 0.99 but also the ones that have *rental_rate* equal to 0.99:

film_id	title	description	release_year	language_id	original_language_id	rental_duration	rental_ra
1	ACADEMY DINOSAUR	A Epic Drama of a Feminist And a Ma...	2006	1	NULL	6	0.99
11	ALAMO VIDEOTAPE	A Boring Epistle of a Butler And a Cat ...	2006	1	NULL	6	0.99
12	ALASKA PHANTOM	A Fanciful Saga of a Hunter And a Pas...	2006	1	NULL	6	0.99
14	ALICE FANTASIA	A Emotional Drama of a A Shark And ...	2006	1	NULL	6	0.99
17	ALONE TRIP	A Fast-Paced Character Study of a C...	2006	1	NULL	3	0.99

Figure 78 – Preview of Output Query with Less than Equal to Example

If we don't provide <= and use <, we'll have a different output:

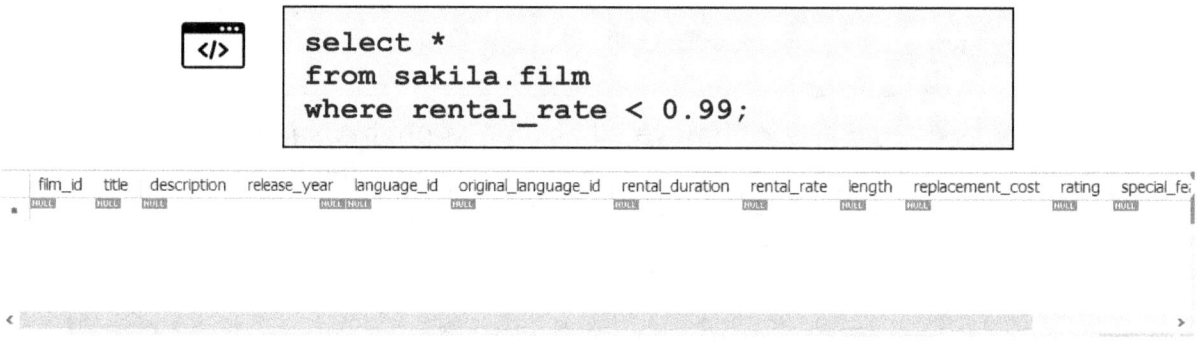

```
select *
from sakila.film
where rental_rate < 0.99;
```

film_id	title	description	release_year	language_id	original_language_id	rental_duration	rental_rate	length	replacement_cost	rating	special_fe
NULL	NULL	NULL	NULL	NULL	NULL	NULL	NULL	NULL	NULL	NULL	NULL

Figure 79 – Preview of Output Query with Less Than Example

No records are retrieved because the minimum rental rate in the table is 0.99. It's important to note that the output consists entirely of **NULL** values because this is MySQL's way of indicating that the query results in an empty set, with no rows returned. Several factors can lead to this, with the most common ones being:

- The table you're attempting to query is empty.
- None of the rows in our table meet the criteria specified in the **WHERE** clause.

In our case, the second scenario happened. Furthermore, you can also employ comparison operators such as 'greater than' or 'greater than or equal to', by flipping the direction of the inequality symbol.

```
select *
from sakila.film
where rental_rate >= 2.99;
```

```
select *
from sakila.film
where rental_rate > 2.99;
```

These two queries translate into:

> "I want all columns from the sakila.film table but only the rows where the rental price is greater than or equal to 2.99"

> "I want all columns from the sakila.film table but only the rows where the rental price is greater than 2.99"

In the output tables from the instructions above, we can see a different number of rows:

⊙	6	00:03:40	select * from sakila.film where rental_rate >= 2.99 LIMIT 0, 10000	659 row(s) returned
⊙	7	00:04:04	select * from sakila.film where rental_rate > 2.99 LIMIT 0, 10000	336 row(s) returned

Figure 80 – Output Statement with Greater Than and Greater Than Equal To

Naturally, the use of the '>=' clause results in a larger output (659 rows) because it includes movies with a rental rate of 2.99 as well. These movies are excluded in the second query, which only employs the '>' operator. In conclusion, mastering the **WHERE** clause in SQL opens the door to powerful and precise data retrieval. Whether filtering rows based on equality, inequality, or employing logical operators like **AND** and **OR**, you can now employ more complex queries, filtering the data with specific criteria.

3.3 New Columns and Calculations

Exclusively relying on the columns available in our tables could limit our capabilities and potentially make our SQL work somewhat dull. Fortunately, we have the flexibility to perform additional calculations, opening up cool possibilities within our data processing. In SQL, we can also create new columns by combining existing information or creating new data, something very neat!

For instance, consider a scenario where we want to introduce a new column that reflects the "*role*" of the person in a movie. In our case, we are going to introduce this column in the *actor* table. First, let's examine the tructure of the table:

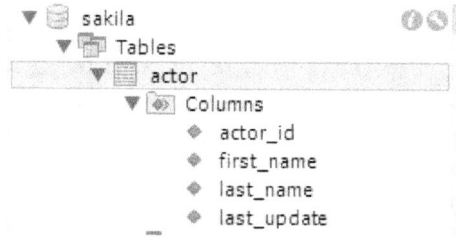

Figure 81 – sakila.actor table structure

The structure we see on Figure 82 can be seen on the navigator on the left of MySQL workbench:

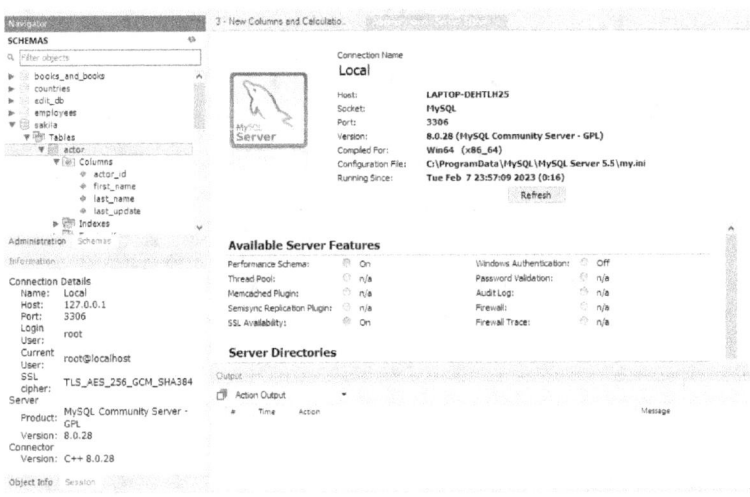

Figure 82 – MySQL Workbench User Interface

This is also the first time we are dealing with the *sakila.actor* table so it's a good idea to preview it first:

```
select *
from sakila.actor;
```

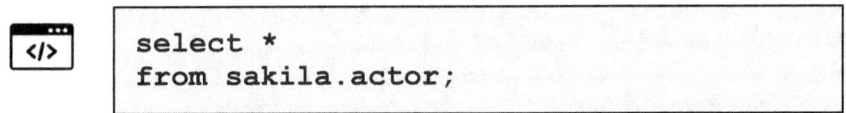

Figure 83 – sakila.actor table

Imagine that we would like to create a new column called *person_role* in this table. To add a new column that doesn't exist in the returning output, we can do the following:

```
select *, 'actor' as person_role
from sakila.actor;
```

This query translates into the following sentence:

I'd like to retrieve all columns from the 'sakila.actor' table, and I want to add a new column called 'person_role' with each row populated with the text 'actor'.

As per tradition, let's break down the query above:

- By using "**select ***," we're informing SQL that we wish to retrieve all the columns from the table specified in the "**from**" clause.
- The unique and noteworthy aspect of this query can be found in the phrase " **'actor' as person_role.**" This instructs SQL to generate a new column in the output labeled "**person_role**" where every value is set to **'actor'**
- To complete the query, we refer to the table from which we want to extract the existing column using "**from sakila.actor**"

This query results in an interesting set:

actor_id	first_name	last_name	last_update	person_role
1	PENELOPE	GUINESS	2006-02-15 04:34:33	actor
2	NICK	WAHLBERG	2006-02-15 04:34:33	actor
3	ED	CHASE	2006-02-15 04:34:33	actor
4	JENNIFER	DAVIS	2006-02-15 04:34:33	actor
5	JOHNNY	LOLLOBRIGIDA	2006-02-15 04:34:33	actor
6	BETTE	NICHOLSON	2006-02-15 04:34:33	actor

Figure 84 – sakila.actor table with new column

SQL Language for Absolute Beginners

Another feature is the ability to generate additional columns by leveraging existing data. As an illustration, we can create a fresh column containing the complete names of actors by utilizing available information about their first and last names:

```
select first_name, last_name, concat(first_name, last_name) as full_name from sakila.actor;
```

This marks our first encounter with an SQL function! The `'concat'` function comes into play here, enabling the combination of `'first_name'` and `'last_name'` columns into a single one. In essence, a SQL function is a command enclosed in parentheses, which allows for the inclusion of specific arguments. For instance, the `'concat()'` function merges multiple strings into a single string.

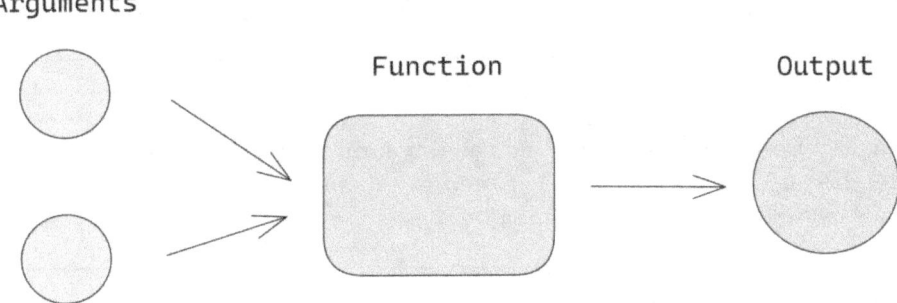

Figure 85 – Illustrative example of a function

In figure 85, we can see the following:

- The green circles are *arguments*. They are fed as input to the function that will use these arguments to do something with them. In our example, **first_name** and **last_name** are being used as such.
- The round rectangle represents the inner workings of a function. These processes take in the arguments and produce some type of output. In our example, this is represented by the **concat** keyword that joins multiple strings together.
- Lastly, the blue circle represents the output, what the function returns.

When we use column names as arguments within the function, it works on each row individually, generating unique outcomes based on the values within those columns.

Let's take a look into our `'full_name'` example:

first_name	last_name	full_name
PENELOPE	GUINESS	PENELOPEGUINESS
NICK	WAHLBERG	NICKWAHLBERG
ED	CHASE	EDCHASE
JENNIFER	DAVIS	JENNIFERDAVIS
JOHNNY	LOLLOBRIGIDA	JOHNNYLOLLOBRIGIDA

Figure 86 – full_name column example

With the query above, we are translating the following sentence into SQL code:

> "I'd like to retrieve the 'first_name,' 'last_name,' and the combined 'first_name' and 'last_name' from the 'sakila.actor' table."

But... there's a slight issue with our newly created column! Can you spot it? The full name is not easily readable because it lacks a space between the names! Can you think of a way to quickly insert this space using the `'concat()'` function?

```
select first_name, last_name, concat(first_name, ' ',
last_name) as full_name from sakila.actor;
```

Simply by adding an additional parameter to the `'concat'` function, we can insert an extra space between the actor's first and last names.

first_name	last_name	full_name
PENELOPE	GUINESS	PENELOPE GUINESS
NICK	WAHLBERG	NICK WAHLBERG
ED	CHASE	ED CHASE
JENNIFER	DAVIS	JENNIFER DAVIS
JOHNNY	LOLLOBRIGIDA	JOHNNY LOLLOBRIGIDA

Figure 87 – full_name column example with three arguments

This is an important takeaway: functions do not necessarily accept only two arguments. They can accommodate any number of arguments, either variable or fixed, depending on the function's purpose. As we progress through the book, we will encounter various examples that will enhance your understanding of this concept. In the case of the `concat` function, the arguments represent the number of strings we intend to combine, allowing the function to accept a potentially infinite number of arguments. It would be impractical to present all the SQL functions available (which exceed a hundred), so this[18] resource aims to provide you with a comprehensive overview. Nevertheless, keep in mind that we will delve into the most renowned functions throughout the book.

Alright, so returning to our new columns and calculations discussion: so far, we've explored two methods for generating new columns:

- Assigning a constant value to populate an entire column (as shown in the `actor` example).
- Employing functions to derive values based on existing columns, resulting in distinct values for the new column depending on the data in each row.

But, we still have to explore another common approach to creating new columns, that involves using mathematical expressions. While the following calculation may not have a practical purpose, let's select a numeric column from our table and perform a mathematical operation on it. For instance, we can multiply `actor_id` by 100 as seen in the next block of code.

```
select *, actor_id * 100
from sakila.actor;
```

actor_id	first_name	last_name	last_update	actor_id * 100
1	PENELOPE	GUINESS	2006-02-15 04:34:33	100
2	NICK	WAHLBERG	2006-02-15 04:34:33	200
3	ED	CHASE	2006-02-15 04:34:33	300
4	JENNIFER	DAVIS	2006-02-15 04:34:33	400
5	JOHNNY	LOLLOBRIGIDA	2006-02-15 04:34:33	500

*Figure 88 – actor_id * 100 example column*

---

[18] https://dev.mysql.com/doc/refman/8.0/en/functions.html

> I'd like to retrieve all columns from the 'sakila.actor' table and include a new column in the result set where each value is derived by multiplying the 'actor_id' by 100.

In this query, we are requesting all columns from the `sakila.actor` table along with the result of the calculation *actor_id* times 100. Apart from multiplication, SQL also allows for the use of other common mathematical expressions, such as:

- '/' for division
- '+' for addition
- '-' for subtraction

Furthermore, SQL adheres to mathematical rules, including the order of operations, as demonstrated in the following code block:

```
select *, actor_id * (100+10)
from sakila.actor;
```

actor_id	first_name	last_name	last_update	actor_id * (100+10)
1	PENELOPE	GUINESS	2006-02-15 04:34:33	110
2	NICK	WAHLBERG	2006-02-15 04:34:33	220
3	ED	CHASE	2006-02-15 04:34:33	330
4	JENNIFER	DAVIS	2006-02-15 04:34:33	440
5	JOHNNY	LOLLOBRIGIDA	2006-02-15 04:34:33	550

*Figure 88 – actor_id * (100+10) example column*

Take note how the calculation (100 + 10) was given priority and executed first. The result was then multiplied by the **actor_id** and this example illustrates the use of the rules of mathematical order of operations, including the use of parentheses, which SQL strictly follows. Furthermore, we can utilize other mathematical functions - for instance, consider computing the logarithm of a number using the '**log**' function.

```
select actor_id, log(actor_id)
from sakila.actor;
```

actor_id	log(actor_id)
58	4.060443010546419
92	4.5217885770490405
182	5.204006687076795
118	4.770684624465665
145	4.976733742420574
194	5.267858159063328

Figure 89 – log(actor_id) example column

In this situation, we create a column with the natural logarithm applied for each **actor_id** number in our dataset. While you don't need to delve into the details of what a natural logarithm means, it's crucial to understand that these kinds of mathematical functions are relevant in the world of SQL. Even though it is illogical in this particular instance (applying a logarithm to an identifier doesn't make much sense), it's essential to be aware that these mathematical functions can be applied to rows containing numerical data.

Another thing stands our in Figure 89 - notice the default and somewhat uninspiring column name '**log(actor_id)**'? How can we make this a bit more meaningful? The answer lies in something we've already learned: an alias. Let's see how to apply one:

```
select actor_id, log(actor_id) as log_actor_id
from sakila.actor;
```

actor_id	log_actor_id
58	4.060443010546419
92	4.5217885770490405
182	5.204006687076795
118	4.770684624465665
145	4.976733742420574
194	5.267858159063328

Figure 90 – log(actor_id) example column using an alias

When we employ an alias to rename a recently generated column, **we substitute the default name with a more descriptive one.** This adds to the arguments of utilizing aliases: incorporating them can contribute to rendering our output more engaging and clear.

Whew! We've covered a bunch of ground in this chapter, from crafting new columns using various methods—whether it's setting constant values or playing with intricate math. It's like turning raw data into a whole new story! But before we dive into the exercises, there's an important bit left to tackle as SQL has more tricks up its sleeve with additional clauses. In the next chapter, we'll dive into three big ones: `GROUP BY`, `ORDER BY`, and `HAVING`. Understanding these clauses will amp up our SQL game, giving us more power to play with data and discover new secrets. So, buckle up for the next chapter—it's going to be quite the ride!

3.4 Additional Query Clauses

Until now, we've delved into three fundamental query clauses in SQL:

- **SELECT**: As we've seen, this clause empowers us to shape the elements within our result set. For instance, it allows us to pick specific columns or generate new ones based on distinct values.
- **FROM**: This clause specifies the table to which our SELECT operation pertains.
- **WHERE**: This clause enables us to filter particular rows from our tables.

After exploring those clauses, we're ready to dig in into another vital query clause known as **GROUP BY**. We'll start with a straightforward example but before that, let's refresh our memory with the *sakila.film* table, shown in Figure 91.

film_id	title	description	release_year	language_id	orig	rental_duration	rental_rate	length	replacement_cost	rating	special_features	last_up
1	ACADEMY...	A Epic Dr...	2006	1	NULL	6	0.99	86	20.99	PG	Deleted Scenes,B...	2006-0
2	ACE GOL...	A Astoun...	2006	1	NULL	3	4.99	48	12.99	G	Trailers,Deleted S...	2006-0
3	ADAPTAT...	A Astoun...	2006	1	NULL	7	2.99	50	18.99	NC-17	Trailers,Deleted S...	2006-0
4	AFFAIR P...	A Fanciful...	2006	1	NULL	5	2.99	117	26.99	G	Commentaries,Be...	2006-0
5	AFRICAN ...	A Fast-Pa...	2006	1	NULL	6	2.99	130	22.99	G	Deleted Scenes	2006-0

Figure 91 – sakila.film example table

Now, let's consider a scenario where we want to retrieve the average rental rate price and the average length of all movies in our table. This can be achieved effortlessly using an aggregation function such as `'avg'`:

```
SELECT avg(rental_rate) as avg_rental_rate,
avg(length) as avg_length
FROM sakila.film;
```

I'd like to obtain the average rental rate and average movie length for all the films in the sakila.film table.

This step marks our first interaction with an aggregator function in SQL Apart from other functions such as the `LOG` or `CONCAT`, aggregator functions become useful when we want to summarize a specific column using a formula. The `'AVG()'` function, for instance, computes the average of the values in the column given in the argument. Here's the outcome of the query above:

avg_rental_rate	avg_length
2.980000	115.2720

Figure 92 – Aggregator function examples

Based on the information shown in Figure 92, the average rental rate for all movies in our table is 2.98, and the average length is 115.2720. The break down of the query above is:

- In the line "`SELECT avg(rental_rate) as avg_rental_rate`" we specify that we want to create the `'avg_rental_rate'` column using the `'avg'` function.

- Similarly, in "`avg(length) as avg_length`" we state our intention to create the `'avg_length'` column using the `'avg'` function.

- The `'FROM sakila.film'`" simply points to the table from which we wish to retrieve the information.

This is neat but what if we wish to explore the average rental rate and length for various movies based on their rating? For example, we might seek to identify if there's a notable contrast in rental rates and lengths based on the movie's rating[19]. This is where the impactful `GROUP BY` clause becomes essential.

```
select rating, avg(rental_rate) as avg_rental_rate,
avg(length) as avg_length
from sakila.film
group by rating;
```

---

[19] Movie ratings are age-based classifications assigned to films by rating boards to guide audiences on the appropriateness of content.

> I'm switching between lower and upper case statements since SQL is generally not case-sensitive in most instructions (except for column and table names). For instance, SQL will treat "SELECT" and "select" in precisely the same manner.

While resembling our prior query, the code above includes a crucial statement that cannot be overlooked—the new clause: **GROUP BY**. To understand this better, let's articulate our query in English:

> I would like to obtain the average rental rate and average length for each distinct Rating from the sakila.film table.

Can you guess what the output of this query is? Let's see:

rating	avg_rental_rate	avg_length
PG	3.051856	112.0052
G	2.888876	111.0506
NC-17	2.970952	113.2286
PG-13	3.034843	120.4439
R	2.938718	118.6615

Figure 93 – Group BY example

In this one, we are calculating distinct averages for both rental rate and length based on each unique movie rating in our table! Although complex to understand at first, GROUP BY is a widely used clause in the SQL language. So, let's take a moment to understand how it works behind the scenes.

If we imagine having only six movies with varying rates, length and rental rate in our database:

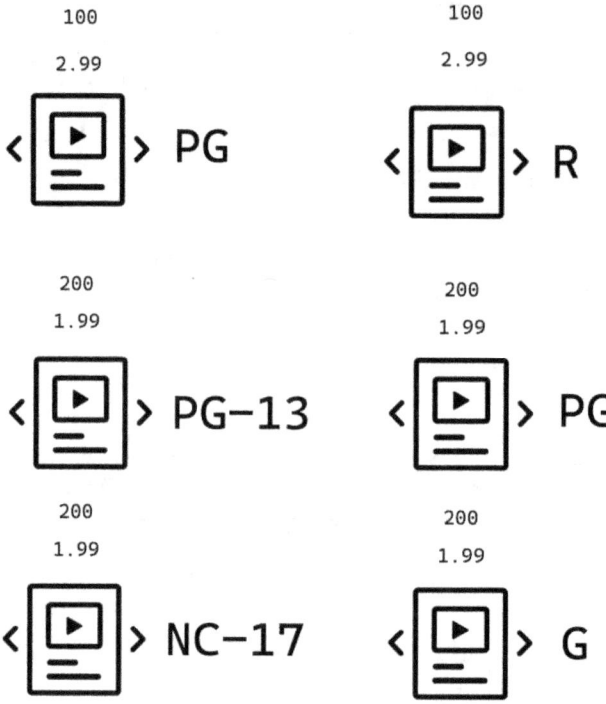

Figure 94 – Group by Example Data

Above each "movie" icon in Figure 94, we showcase their corresponding length and rental rate, with the movie rating positioned directly beside the icon. For example, the initial movie in the upper-left corner is rated PG, has a duration of 100 minutes, and carries a rental rate of $2.99. When employing **GROUP BY** on a column, SQL begins by categorizing the elements based on the specified column in the clause. In our scenario, we will group all movies with the same rating together, as illustrated in Figure 95.

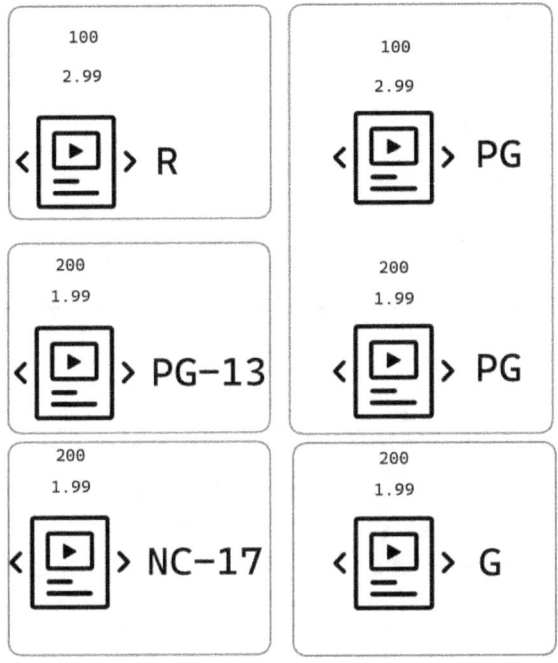

Figure 95 – Grouped Data example

Now, with the grouped movies, we can compute the average movie lengths for each rating type:

- Movies R rating have an average of $2.99 rental rate and 100 minutes (only one movie with this rating in our database).
- Average of a $1.99 rental rate and 200 minutes for movies with a PG-13 rating (only one movie in our data).
- Average of a $1.99 rental rate and 200 minutes for movies with an NC-17 rating (only one movie in our data).
- Average of a $1.99 rental rate and 200 minutes for movies with a G rating (only one movie in our data).
- For the PG movies, we have to do something different. Has we have two movies of this kind, we need to calculate the average of the rental rates *(2.99 and 1.99)* and lengths *(100 and 200)* – in this case, we sum the values and divide by two, calculating the average of both length and rental rate.

The aggregator function has the ability to apply a function to each set of data grouped by the variable specified in the **GROUP BY** clause, automating this calculation process.

Another important detail is the importance of including the **GROUP BY** variable in the **SELECT** clause. Without it, we may encounter difficulties in associating distinct values, such as ratings, with their respective averages. For example:

```
select avg(rental_rate) as avg_rental_rate,
avg(length) as avg_length
from sakila.film
group by rating;
```

avg_rental_rate	avg_length
3.051856	112.0052
2.888876	111.0506
2.970952	113.2286
3.034843	120.4439
2.938718	118.6615

Figure 96 – Grouped Data example without stating the variable in the SELECT statement

In this example, it becomes quite challenging to discern the specific Rating to which the average rental rate and length refer to. Incorporating the variable mentioned in the **GROUP BY** into the **SELECT** clause mitigates this as seen in Figure 93.

Now, consider the scenario where we wish to retrieve only the ratings with an average rental rate exceeding 3. Can a **WHERE** clause be employed? Let's explore the outcome of applying the familiar filter clause we've learned:

```
select rating, avg(rental_rate) as avg_rental_rate
from sakila.film
where avg_rental_rate>3
group by rating;
```

Oh no! Unfortunately we have an error in our code, as shown in Figure 97.

Error Code: 1054. Unknown column 'avg_rental_rate' in 'where clause'

Figure 97 – Error on WHERE clause

What happened? Well, mainly this happened because a very important rule in SQL: the **WHERE** clause is implemented BEFORE any computations in the query. **Understanding this fundamental rule in SQL is crucial, particularly when dealing with more sophisticated queries.**

Since the `avg_rental_rate` column is computed within the query, it cannot be accessed using a **WHERE** clause. Fortunately, there's an alternative clause that allows us to address this issue - the **HAVING** clause:

```
select rating, avg(rental_rate) as avg_rental_rate
from sakila.film
group by rating
having avg_rental_rate > 3;
```

rating	avg_rental_rate
PG	3.051856
PG-13	3.034843

Figure 98 – HAVING clause example result

How can we translate this clause into English? Let's see:

I aim to retrieve both the rating and its corresponding average rental rate for each distinct rating. However, I only wish to display the ratings whose average rental rate exceeds 3.

> The WHERE clause takes effect prior to any computations in our query. When dealing with a column generated within our query, the appropriate clause to use is the HAVING clause.

To illustrate the limitation of **WHERE** in accessing columns created during the query, let's attempt to generate a column with an alias and filter values using that newly assigned column name. For instance, consider the following query to start

```
select film_id, rating as movie_rating
from sakila.film;
```

film_id	movie_rating
1	PG
2	G
3	NC-17
4	G
5	G
6	PG

Figure 99 – Film_id and Rating preview Rows

Now let's pick up the exact same query and try to select all movies with rating = 'PG' using **WHERE** and the alias *movie_rating* we've just coded:

```
select film_id, rating as movie_rating
from sakila.film
where movie_rating= 'PG';
```

Error Code: 1054. Unknown column 'movie_rating' in 'where clause'

Figure 100 – Error on WHERE clause – movie_rating example

The problem with this code is similar to the one we encountered previously. The column `movie_rating` is generated during the query (**even though the data is pre-existing, the column name undergoes transformation during the query**). While the rating column does exist in the underlying table, the name `movie_rating` is unfamiliar to SQL before the query starts.

So what's the solution? Exactly... **HAVING** clause!

```
select film_id, rating as movie_rating
from sakila.film
having movie_rating= 'PG';
```

film_id	movie_rating
1	PG
6	PG
12	PG
13	PG
19	PG
37	PG

Figure 101 – HAVING result example – filter PG movies

Since we're employing a filter with **HAVING** this time, SQL can understand the term `movie_rating` and appropriately filter our table. As this is a very important concept in the language, let me provide another example for clarification.

```
select rating, avg(rental_rate) as avg_rental_rate
from sakila.film
where rental_rate > 1.99
group by rating;
```

rating	avg_rental_rate
G	3.954912
NC-17	4.026496
PG	4.020303
PG-13	4.009868
R	4.030000

Figure 102 – GROUP BY result example – filter all movies with rental rate over 1.99

The **WHERE** clause in this instance narrows down the selection to movies with a rental rate exceeding 1.99 **before** grouping the data. Essentially, it focuses solely on examples that meet this criterion when performing the group by aggregation but it does not filter the ratings with average rental rate lower than 1.99. As we are filtering movies before the calculation is applied, the **WHERE** clause works here. Remember that **HAVING** only comes into play after grouping the instances. **Keep in mind that this mirrors the sequence of these clauses in the SELECT statement as WHERE always comes before HAVING.**

Now, before delving into the initial exercise section, let's briefly explore the last query clause: **ORDER BY**. **ORDER BY** has the capability to arrange the query result based on a specific column, as demonstrated in the following example.

```
select title, description, length
from sakila.film
order by length;
```

title	description	length
ALIEN CENTER	A Brilliant Drama of a Cat And a Mad Scientist w...	46
IRON MOON	A Fast-Paced Documentary of a Mad Cow And ...	46
KWAI HOMEWARD	A Amazing Drama of a Car And a Squirrel who m...	46
LABYRINTH LEAGUE	A Awe-Inspiring Saga of a Composer And a Fris...	46
RIDGEMONT SUBMARINE	A Unbelieveable Drama of a Waitress And a Co...	46
DIVORCE SHINING	A Unbelieveable Saga of a Crocodile And a Stud...	47
DOWNHILL ENOUGH	A Emotional Tale of a Pastry Chef And a Forensi...	47

Figure 103 – ORDER BY result example

In this query, we're arranging the resulting table in ascending order based on the length column with shorter movies showing up first in the result. The **ORDER BY** clause appears at the end of the query statement, and in the query mentioned earlier, we're requesting the following:

"I want to choose the title, description, and length from the sakila.film table, with the outcome arranged in ascending order based on the length of the movies."

Naturally, we can also sort these elements in descending order. This is achieved by providing an extra keyword **DESC** after the **ORDER BY** statement:

```
select title, description, length
from sakila.film
order by length desc;
```

The only variation in this query is that the resulting output displays all movies arranged in descending order, beginning with the longest movies first, as illustrated in figure 104.

title	description	length
CHICAGO NORTH	A Fateful Yarn of a Mad Cow And a Waitress w...	185
CONTROL ANTHEM	A Fateful Documentary of a Robot And a Stude...	185
DARN FORRESTER	A Fateful Story of a A Shark And a Explorer wh...	185
GANGS PRIDE	A Taut Character Study of a Woman And a A S...	185
HOME PITY	A Touching Panorama of a Man And a Secret Ag...	185
MUSCLE BRIGHT	A Stunning Panorama of a Sumo Wrestler And a...	185
POND SEATTLE	A Stunning Drama of a Teacher And a Boat who...	185

Figure 104 – ORDER BY DESC example

Concluding this section on fundamental SQL queries, we've understood the 6 most essential query clauses. Within this section, we've covered:

- SELECT
- FROM
- WHERE

- GROUP BY
- HAVING
- ORDER BY

Now, as we transition to the exercise section of this book, it's crucial to underscore the importance of hands-on practice in your learning journey. SQL, much like any other language, is most effectively mastered through consistent application and experimentation. The provided exercises will act as stepping stones, progressively enhancing your proficiency and confidence in constructing complex SQL queries. Invest time in understand the problem statement and breaking it down into smaller, manageable tasks. As you advance, you'll encounter challenges that demand critical thinking, utilizing the knowledge acquired from the chapters. Remember, the path to mastering SQL is an ongoing process of learning and refining your skills!

Throughout the exercises, challenge yourself to explore different ways of solving the problems using queries. Experiment with alternative query structures, test out various functions and operators, and compare the efficiency of different approaches. Getting hands on with the language will be the only to help you improve further so without further delay, let's jump into our first exercise section!

3.5 Exercise Section

In this coding exercise segment, you can apply what we've covered about our query clauses so far. To engage with a practice dataset distinct from the *sakila* database, let's begin by running a script that will generate the table we'll use throughout this exercise section – open MYSQL and a new script to run the code below:

```
CREATE DATABASE exercises;

CREATE TABLE exercises.transactions (transaction_id integer,
product_name varchar(10), price float, discount float,
product_category varchar(20));

INSERT INTO exercises.transactions (
    transaction_id, product_name, price, discount, product_category
)
  VALUES (1, "Toy Car", 2, 0, "Toys"),
         (2, "Toy Box", 200, 0, "Toys"),
         (3, "Jacket", 79, 0, "Clothes"),
         (4, "Blouse", 80, 20, "Clothes");
```

Don't worry about the instructions behind this query. It's essentially a script used exclusively to create our practice table and we'll learn all techniques behind it during chapter 5. But the goal here is to create a table to work with during the exercises, so don't worry too much about the details of the query right now.

Figure 105 – Result from running code related to exercises.transactions

If you see lines similar to the ones shown in Figure 105 on the Output window, the table *transactions* has been successfully created and you are good to go!

3.5.1 Exercises

1. Select all the transactions where the **product_category** is equal to **"Toys"**. Select all the columns also.

2. Select all the transactions where the **price** is > 10 or the **category** is not equal to "Toys". Select all the columns also.

3. Select all the columns in the **transactions** table plus create a column where you subtract the **discount** from the **price**. Call this column **price_minus_discount**

4. Sum all the prices by Product Category from the transactions table but only consider products that cost more than 10 dollars. Call the summed prices column **sum_price**.

5. Select the **product_name** from the **transactions** table and order the result by this column, in descending order.

3.5.2 Exercise Solutions

Next to all exercises, I'll always show the solutions in the format below. Each answer number corresponds to the solution to the question with the same number in the section right before this one.

1. ```
select * from exercises.transactions where product_category =
'Toys';
```

2. ```
select * from exercises.transactions where (price > 10) or
(product_category != 'Toys');
```

3. ```
select *, price-discount as price_minus_discount from
exercises.transactions;
```

4. ```
select product_category, sum(price) as sum_price
from exercises.transactions
where price > 10
group by product_category;
```

5. ```
select product_name
from exercises.transactions
order by product_name desc
```
```

4. SQL Data Types

Alright! So after studying query basics, it's time to expand our knowledge in SQL. Query basic clauses are important because they serve as the foundation for more advanced database operations in the language. Understanding the basic clauses is like mastering the alphabet before delving into complex sentence structures. The query clauses, including **SELECT, FROM, WHERE, GROUP BY, HAVING,** and **ORDER BY**, provide essential building blocks for crafting queries that retrieve, filter, group, and sort data. As you advance in SQL, **you'll discover that these fundamental clauses are not just isolated concepts but interweave to create more advanced queries that can manipulate data in versatile ways.** Speaking of versatile, did you notice that we've worked with a lot of different data types in the past chapter? We've seen integer and float numbers (for example, the *film_id* or the *rental rate* of the movie) and even text, such as the *name* of the actor.

Like many programming languages, SQL effectively manages the data it stores through the use of data types. Properly defining and handling data types is crucial to prevent bugs and efficiently manage resources within SQL databases. They play a crucial role for two main reasons:

- They determine how our data is physically stored in the computer's memory.
- They dictate the types of functions we can apply to our columns. For instance, it's typical that we can't perform a sum or average function on columns with character (text) data types.

To illustrate data types, let's start by executing the **DESCRIBE** command on one of our tables. This command provides extensive information about the underlying data stored in each table. For example, to describe the '*sakila.film*' table, we use the following command:

```
DESCRIBE sakila.film;
```

Field	Type	Null	Key	Default	Extra
film_id	smallint unsigned	NO	PRI	NULL	auto_increment
title	varchar(128)	NO	MUL	NULL	
description	text	YES		NULL	
release_year	year	YES		NULL	
language_id	tinyint unsigned	NO	MUL	NULL	
original_language_id	tinyint unsigned	YES	MUL	NULL	
rental_duration	tinyint unsigned	NO		3	
rental_rate	decimal(4,2)	NO		4.99	

Figure 106 – DESCRIBE example

"I want to describe the sakila.film table, retrieving information about the table's columns."

The **DESCRIBE** command details information about a specific table. In Figure 106, we can observe important details regarding the *sakila.film* table. Although this table may appear a bit difficult to understand, by the end of the book, every aspect of it should become clearer. Nevertheless, let me shed a light on each column of the **DESCRIBE** output presented above:

- Field: This column contains the name of each column in the *sakila.film* table.
- Type: This column specifies the data type the column holds and provides additional properties.
- Null: Indicates whether the column allows NULL values.
- Key: Specifies whether the column serves as a key for the table.
- Default: Reveals if the column has a default value, in case no value is provided when populating the rows.
- Extra: Provides additional properties about the column.

This type of data about data is commonly referred to as *metadata*.

The term "metadata" is a widely used expression that denotes information about data. As an illustration, the DESCRIBE command retrieves information about the columns present in our tables.

Throughout the remainder of this chapter, our attention will be directed towards the *Type* column featured in Figure 106. This column indicates the data type that each column, as specified in the "field," is capable of holding. For example, the *title* column can store data with a **varchar** data type, allowing for the inclusion of characters — this is a logical choice for movie titles, often represented by written text.

Examining the Type in Figure 106, and setting aside the "**unsigned**" keyword for now (we'll delve into its meaning shortly), we encounter six distinct data types:

- **smallint**
- **varchar**
- **text**

- **year**
- **tinyint**
- **decimal**

The various data types serve distinct purposes as they have the capacity to accommodate different values. Let's delve into the details of some of them and examine the implications of opting for one over the others.

4.1. Numeric Data Types

Numeric data types have the ability to store values of any numerical nature, allowing for the execution of mathematical calculations. For instance, consider the scenario where we contemplate raising prices in our movie rental shop by multiplying the current prices by 4 (although I would strongly advise against such a move, as it could potentially result in significant customer loss!). In the *sakila.film*, accomplishing this task is quite straightforward as we can easily multiply the prices by incorporating a formula into the **SELECT** statement.

```
select film_id, rental_rate,
rental_rate*4 as calc
from sakila.film;
```

film_id	rental_rate	calc
1	0.99	3.96
2	4.99	19.96
3	2.99	11.96
4	2.99	11.96
5	2.99	11.96
6	2.99	11.96
7	4.99	19.96
8	4.99	19.96

Figure 107– Calculated column example.

Here, we're creating a new column named "**calc**" which holds the value resulting from multiplying the **rental_rate** by 4. In SQL, the multiplication operation is denoted by the asterisk (*****) symbol.[20]

---

[20] Other common mathematical operations like addition (+), subtraction (-), or division (/) can be applied to columns with numeric data types.

This type of operation is exclusive to columns created with a numeric data type. What happens when we attempt to apply multiplication to a column containing different data types? For instance, if we attempt to multiply a column containing **text** (represented by the text data type), it would lead to either an error or a nonsensical result:

```
select film_id, title, title*4 as calc
from sakila.film;
```

film_id	title	calc
1	ACADEMY DINOSAUR	0
2	ACE GOLDFINGER	0
3	ADAPTATION HOLES	0
4	AFFAIR PREJUDICE	0
5	AFRICAN EGG	0
6	AGENT TRUMAN	0
7	AIRPLANE SIERRA	0
8	AIRPORT POLLOCK	0

Figure 108 – Calculated column example with text column.

The resulting calculation lacks significance, as we end up with 0 for every row. In essence, MySQL indicates that it cannot execute this operation, yielding an output that holds no meaningful value. Moreover, the numeric nature of the column allows us to employ more advanced mathematical functions. Let's calculate the logarithm[21] of the column, through the use of the **log** function.

```
select film_id, rental_rate,
log(rental_rate) as calc
from sakila.film;
```

---

[21] You don't need to worry too much about what "logarithm" means here.

film_id	rental_rate	calc
1	0.99	-0.01005033585350145
2	4.99	1.6074359097634274
3	2.99	1.095273387402595
4	2.99	1.095273387402595
5	2.99	1.095273387402595
6	2.99	1.095273387402595
7	4.99	1.6074359097634274
8	4.99	1.6074359097634274

Figure 109 – Calculation of logarithm of a numeric column.

And, naturally, when you apply a logarithm to a column of text, the outcome turns out rather peculiar:

```
select film_id, title, log(title) as calc
from sakila.film;
```

film_id	title	calc
1	ACADEMY DINOSAUR	NULL
2	ACE GOLDFINGER	NULL
3	ADAPTATION HOLES	NULL
4	AFFAIR PREJUDICE	NULL
5	AFRICAN EGG	NULL
6	AGENT TRUMAN	NULL
7	AIRPLANE SIERRA	NULL
8	AIRPORT POLLOCK	NULL

Figure 110 – Calculation of logarithm of a text column.

This generates a new value that we haven't previously encountered. This renowned value is infamous for causing headaches in SQL tasks and is commonly known as **NULL**. It means missing information or can arise from an invalid computation, posing a significant challenge to manage. In this particular scenario, when we attempt to calculate the logarithm of a text variable, it lacks logical coherence, prompting SQL to return this value as an indication of an invalid computation. Certain straightforward computations on text columns yield **0**, while more complex functions yield **NULL**. You need not delve too deeply into the specifics; just understand that SQL generates these strange outcomes due to the data type of the variable.

Now, we know that both numeric and text variables can be stored in SQL columns. But do we have a single way to store them individually? Or are there multiple "numeric" and "text" data types? For instance, by checking the **DESCRIBE** command of our *sakila.film* table, various data types like **smallint**, **tinyint**, or **decimal** can be used to represent data. Why are they different?

Field	Type	Null	Key	Default	Extra
film_id	smallint unsigned	NO	PRI	NULL	auto_increment
title	varchar(128)	NO	MUL	NULL	
description	text	YES		NULL	
release_year	year	YES		NULL	
language_id	tinyint unsigned	NO	MUL	NULL	
original_language_id	tinyint unsigned	YES	MUL	NULL	
rental_duration	tinyint unsigned	NO		3	
rental_rate	decimal(4,2)	NO		4.99	

Figure 111 – Describing the sakila.film table.

Typically, when we're weighing different options for storing numerical data, there are two key considerations:

- What range of values do we anticipate storing in our column?
- What level of precision do we want to maintain when storing our numerical data?

To illustrate, nothing better than delving into the characteristics of various numerical data types available in SQL:

- **bit** (binary or boolean value): stores either 1 or 0 values.
- **tinyint**: accommodates numbers from 0 to 255.
- **smallint**: handles integers within the range of -32,768 to 32,767.
- **int**: manages integers ranging from -2,147,483,648 to 2,147,483,647.
- **bigint**: supports an extensive range of integer values, surpassing int.
- **decimal/numeric**: capable of storing floating-point numbers, with decimal places.
- **float:** also stores floating-point values but is slightly less 'precise' compared to the aforementioned data types.

When deciding which data type to use, it's important to choose the one that can store the necessary range of values while also minimizing storage requirements. In other words, we should opt for a data type that can accommodate the expected range of values without occupying unnecessary storage space.

Let's think about integer columns - why not just use **bigint** for all integer columns? The main reason lies in the potential for unnecessary space consumption on our computer or server, particularly when dealing with extensive databases as SQL allocates the needed space even if we just store a small range of values in the column.

Let's illustrate this with an example: consider a column meant for storing language codes (like *language_id*) of our movies; it's highly improbable that we'd need to accommodate more than 255 language codes. In such instances, opting for a smaller data type, such as `tinyint` (capable of handling values up to 255), makes more sense. This decision optimizes storage space, especially when anticipating a maximum of 255 different languages for our movie records. However, there's a trade-off when using a smaller data type. If, by chance, a value higher than 255 is stored in this `tinyint` column, it triggers a SQL error, as we will see in the future. It's essential to carefully plan your data types!

This past chapter was just a small introduction on numeric data types and we'll have ample opportunity to explore them – particularly when we create our own tables on chapter 5. For now, let's delve deeper into other data types available in the language—specifically, those designed for storing text (also referred to as string) variables!

4.2. Text Data Types

Yet another frequently used set of data types in SQL systems is known as string/character data types. These columns play a crucial role in storing free-text data, and much like numeric data types, there are specific functions applicable only to these data types. Take, for instance, the **concat** function, which effectively combines two pieces of text:

```
select title, concat(title, title) as calc
from sakila.film;
```

In the query mentioned earlier, we're requesting information from the title column and introducing a new column named `'calc'` which combines the displayed title value by repeating it twice, as seen in Figure 112.

Figure 112 – Creating a column with a calculation on a text column.

The **concat** function merges one or more text data columns into a unified one. In our (hypothetical) example, for the initial movie *ACADEMY DINOSAUR*, utilizing **concat(title, title)** yields *ACADEMY DINOSAURACADEMY DINOSAUR*. While the **concat** function specifically operates with text data, applying it to a numeric column triggers SQL to undergo an **implicit conversion** for concatenation of the values:

```
select title, concat(rental_rate, rental_rate) as calc
from sakila.film;
```

title	calc
AIRPLANE SIERRA	4.994.99
AIRPORT POLLOCK	4.994.99
ALABAMA DEVIL	2.992.99
ALADDIN CALENDAR	4.994.99
ALAMO VIDEOTAPE	0.990.99
ALASKA PHANTOM	0.990.99
ALI FOREVER	4.994.99
ALICE FANTASIA	0.990.99

Figure 113 – Implicit conversion example

The term "**implicit conversion**" in SQL denotes a process wherein the system automatically carries out a type conversion without the need for explicit instructions. SQL performs this operation in various scenarios, for example when converting numerical data into text data as necessary. This concept sees widespread use across different programming languages and finds applications in diverse situations.

Let's focus on the initial row in the table shown in Figure 113. Here, we encounter the movie titled "Airplane Sierra" with a value of "4.994.99". This result stems from duplicating the numerical value of 4.99. Initially, the decimal number 4.99 undergoes conversion to a character representation, "4.99". Even though it looks the same visually, the implicit conversion transforms the numeric value 4.99 into a purely textual format and consequently, this character value can undergo concatenation, resulting in the final value of "4.994.99".

Columns with the potential to contain non-numeric characters are well-suited for a text data type, offering flexibility for storing unstructured text. For example, names of people, addresses or location names are some of the most common usages where text data types are used. However, it's crucial to be mindful that these data types may consume a significant amount of storage space on a computer or server.

In SQL, various text data types are at our disposal, including:

- The **TEXT** data type, which accommodates free text up to a maximum of 65,535 bytes (not characters, as encoding may influence byte count per character).
- **VARCHAR**, similar to **TEXT**, but can be utilized with indexing.
- **SET** and **ENUM**, resembling each other, permit the use of predefined values to populate a column. **SET** allows for multiple values, while **ENUM** allows only one.

In upcoming sections, we'll explore the opportunity to define our own data types and delve further into working with text data types. Before that, let's delve into another crucial category of data types in SQL – dates!

4.3. Date Data Types

In addition to strings and integers, dates represent another commonly encountered data type in our tables. Within our *sakila.film* table, two columns relate to "time" based variables: the year of the film release and the last update date of the row. Let's examine them with a query:

```
select title, release_year,
last_update
from sakila.film;
```

title	release_year	last_update
ACADEMY DINOSAUR	2006	2006-02-15 05:03:42
ACE GOLDFINGER	2006	2006-02-15 05:03:42
ADAPTATION HOLES	2006	2006-02-15 05:03:42
AFFAIR PREJUDICE	2006	2006-02-15 05:03:42
AFRICAN EGG	2006	2006-02-15 05:03:42
AGENT TRUMAN	2006	2006-02-15 05:03:42
AIRPLANE SIERRA	2006	2006-02-15 05:03:42
AIRPORT POLLOCK	2006	2006-02-15 05:03:42

Figure 114 – Date related columns

These two columns employ distinct data types. The **release_year** column is a **YEAR** type variable that holds the release year of the movie. Conversely, **last_update** contains a timestamp reflecting the last update row of the movie. An important distinction between the two columns is evident: while both contain date-related information, their formats are vastly different. **last_update** displays a timestamp format, incorporating hours, minutes, and seconds, whereas **release_year** solely presents information about the year.

When a column contains date-related information, we can apply very cool functions to it. For instance, we can calculate the difference (in days) between two dates using a function called **datediff**:

```
select datediff("2020-09-01", "2020-10-01");
```

	datediff("2020-09-01", "2020-10-01")
▶	-30

Figure 115 – Difference (in days) between two dates

The **datediff** function provides the variance in the number of days between two dates specified in the function argument. It's worth noting that in the query above, we don't include a **FROM** clause—a specific case in SQL that we can employ when we're not selecting any columns or table in the SQL statement.

> I want the difference (in days) between the 1st of September of 2020 and the 1st of October of 2020

Notice that SQL presents the results in the form of a table with a single row and column. This mirrors the outcome when we perform basic calculations on values without incorporating a **FROM** clause. Additionally, we have the option to modify the name of this single column by employing an alias, as illustrated below:

```
select datediff("2020-09-01", "2020-10-01") as dif;
```

	dif
▶	-30

Figure 116 – Difference (in days) between two dates using an alias

Don't worry too much about the format of this output or why we only see a row and column. Right now, the most important is that you focused on how to use dates in SQL. While we enclose the values within quotes, SQL, upon receiving dates enclosed in these quotes, automatically converts them to a date format before executing the calculation. To illustrate, if we attempt to use the **datediff** function with other values that are purely text, such as 'A' and 'B', we will naturally encounter a strange value in the output (and a familiar one!).

```
select datediff("A", "B") as dif;
```

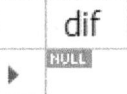

Figure 117 – Difference (in days) between two letters

In this case, a **NULL** value is produced since a date difference cannot be determined between the values 'A' and 'B'. This scenario underscores a crucial principle we've explored in SQL over the recent pages: **data types dictate the types of functions that can be employed on a particular value or column. They also change the expected output of any calculation.** What occurs if we attempt to use **datediff** on an integer value?

```
select datediff(150000, 1545222) as dif;
```

A NULL value, as well! This data type also doesn't align with the **datediff** function.

Figure 118 – Difference (in days) between two integers

Within MySQL, various data types related to dates are available for storing and managing date and time values. Below are the frequently encountered date data types:

- **DATE**: This type is employed to store dates in the 'YYYY-MM-DD' format, representing a date range spanning from '1000-01-01' to '9999-12-31'. The **DATE** data type occupies 3 bytes in size.
- **TIMESTAMP**: This data type is utilized for storing date and time values, resembling **DATETIME** with the format *'YYYY-MM-DD HH:MM:SS'*. However, **TIMESTAMP** has a more limited range, spanning from '1970-01-01 00:00:01' UTC[22] to '2038-01-19 03:14:07' UTC. It's essential to note that internally, **TIMESTAMP** values are stored in UTC but are converted to the current time zone upon retrieval. The **TIMESTAMP** data type occupies 4 bytes.

---

[22] https://en.wikipedia.org/wiki/Coordinated_Universal_Time

- **TIME**: Used for storing time values in the 'HH:MM:SS' format, this data type covers a range from '-838:59:59' to '838:59:59'. The **TIME** data type has a size of 3 bytes.

- **YEAR**: Designed for storing year values in either 2-digit or 4-digit formats ('*YY*' or '*YYYY*'), the **YEAR** data type encompasses a range from 1901 to 2155. Its size is 1 byte.

Furthermore, MySQL offers variations of these data types, such as **DATETIME**(6) and **TIMESTAMP**(6), enabling the storage of fractional seconds with a precision of up to 6 digits.

Concluding this chapter: we've dived into the realm of date-related data types within SQL, expanding our understanding beyond strings and integers. From understanding the distinctions between data types like YEAR and TIMESTAMP to employing functions like `datediff` for calculating date differences, we've navigated through practical examples that helped us shed a light on the versatility of MySQL in handling temporal data. Before going to the exercises, there's one last aspect regarding data types that I want to show you – recall the implicit conversions we encountered in some examples? Well, the setting of data types in tables isn't rigid; we have the capability to employ conversion operators for explicit translations between data types! To delve into this further, let's introduce two vital functions in the language – **CAST** and **CONVERT**!

4.4. Converting Columns

Sometimes, the data types assigned to our columns may not align with the operations we intend to carry out on them. This mismatch can occur due to shortcomings in data modeling[23] or changes in the underlying data. Let's revisit our '*sakila.film*' table, focusing on the '*title*' column that stores movie titles:

```
select title
from sakila.film;
```

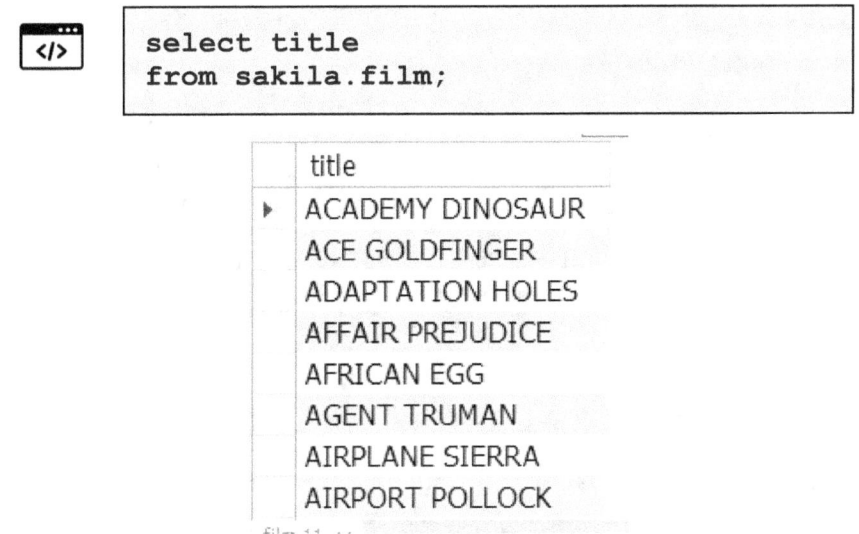

Figure 119 – Title Column from Sakila.film table

We can attempt to convert this column into an integer using the **CAST** function in SQL Naturally, the outcome won't carry much significance since we're converting a column with text data into an integer:

```
select title, CAST(title AS SIGNED INTEGER) as
converted_title
from sakila.film;
```

---

[23] The process of thinking beforehand the data types that our columns should have.

	title	converted_title
▶	ACADEMY DINOSAUR	0
	ACE GOLDFINGER	0
	ADAPTATION HOLES	0
	AFFAIR PREJUDICE	0
	AFRICAN EGG	0
	AGENT TRUMAN	0

Figure 120 – Title Column and Conversion to Integer

Here's a breakdown of the SQL code above:

- In the initial part of the **SELECT** statement, we retrieve the *'title'* column.

- The next column in the **SELECT** statement, we pick the *'title,'* but this time it's passed within a **CAST** function: **CAST(title AS SIGNED INTEGER)**.

- The **CAST** function returns the *'title'* column with the data converted to a **SIGNED INTEGER**. The **'SIGNED'** aspect means that this integer can accommodate negative values. An alias is used to rename the converted column as *'converted_title'*.

The query result will feature two columns: *'title'* preserving the original values, and *'converted_title'* holding the title values as signed integers. Essentially, SQL attempts to convert each title into a numbers, resulting in "0" for movie titles containing text data. Such conversions to integers are more pertinent when dealing with text data containing numeric portions. For instance, imagine airplane seat numbers with formats like "A34" that are stored in a data type accommodating free text. If we aim to convert the numeric part into integers, the process involves using string manipulation functions like **SUBSTRING()** to extract the numeric part of the seat number, followed by using **CAST()** or **CONVERT()** to turn it into an integer data type.

Additionally, we can perform the reverse operation. As an example, let's convert the rental rate to a **TEXT** variable using the **CAST** function:

```
select rental_rate, CAST(rental_rate as CHAR) as
converted_rental_rate
from sakila.film;
```

	rental_rate	converted_rental_rate
▶	0.99	0.99
	4.99	4.99
	2.99	2.99
	2.99	2.99
	2.99	2.99
	2.99	2.99
	4.99	4.99

Figure 121 – Rental Rate Column and Conversion to Text

In this case, SQL successfully converted the column to text, considering that 0.99 can be interpreted as a group of characters. **It's crucial to note that, although we observe the same numeric value in the *'converted_rental_rate'* column, this column will function like any other text column.** A noteworthy aspect of **CAST** is that certain data types cannot be cast (physical table alterations are required to achieve the desired outcome – more details on this shortly!). For instance:

```
select rental_rate, CAST(rental_rate as VARCHAR) as
converted_rental_rate
from sakila.film;
```

When we cast into a **VARCHAR**, we have an error in MYSQL and we can't convert our variable.

Error Code: 1064. You have an error in your SQL syntax; check the manual that correspon...

Figure 122 – Error when Casting to VarChar

The data types that can undergo conversions are the following:

- **BINARY**
- **CHAR**
- **DATE**
- **DATETIME**
- **TIME**
- **DECIMAL**
- **INTEGER**

The journey through data types in the past chapters has provided us with invaluable insights into how information is stored, manipulated, and understood within SQL systems. From numeric data types facilitating mathematical computations to text data types accommodating unstructured information, and finally, to date data types handling temporal aspects, we've explored the diverse landscape of data representation in databases.

As we prepare to embark on exercises to solidify our understanding, remember that the choice of data type is not merely a technical detail but a strategic decision with significant implications for storage efficiency, computational capabilities, and data integrity. Although this may seem confusing at this time, I'm positively sure that the data types concept will also be clearer when we start to create our own tables and information, something we will do next.

As usual, let's dive into the exercises and apply our newfound knowledge to practical scenarios, reinforcing our understanding and honing our skills in SQL mastery!

4.5. Exercise Section

In this coding exercise section, you will be able to practice what we've learned about data types until now. As in the past exercise section, we'll start by executing a script that will create the table we will need to query throughout this exercise section:

```
CREATE TABLE exercises.customers (customer_id integer, customer_name
varchar(30), customer_age integer, birth_date varchar(10),
country_code varchar(4));

INSERT INTO exercises.customers (
    customer_id, customer_name, customer_age, birth_date, country_code
)
 VALUES (1, "John", 25, '1995-09-01', "123"),
       (2, "Anne", 45, 0, '1975-10-04', "324"),
        (3, "Melissa", 21, 0, '1999-04-23', "324"),
        (4, "Charles", 60, 20, '1960-08-22', "123");
```

If this code executed correctly, continue to 4.5.1. If not, you may have encountered a "database doesn't exist" error. This happens because you haven't executed the code in Exercise Section 3.5. To ensure the code above functions properly, execute the command: "**CREATE DATABASE exercises;**" and then try to run the code once more.

4.5.1. Exercises

1. Use a select statement to convert the **customer_age** column into a **varchar(20)** - only show the converted column in the result and call it **convert_cust_age**

2. Use a select statement to convert the **birth_date** column into a date - only show that converted column in the result and call it **convert_birth_date**.

3. Use a select statement to select the customer_id and convert the **country_code** column into a integer - only show both columns in the result and call the converted column **convert_country_code**.

4.5.2. Exercise Solutions

1. ```
select cast(customer_age as varchar(20)) as convert_cust_age
from exercises.customers;
```

2. ```
select cast(birth_date as date) as convert_birth_date from
exercises.customers;
```

3. ```
select customer_id, cast(country_code as integer) as
convert_country_code from exercises.customers;
```
```

5. Creating and Modifying Tables

Until now, we've exclusively employed tables that were pre-existing in our databases. To illustrate, in the initial chapter of the book, we generated our *sakila* database using a somewhat mysterious script capable of crafting both the database and tables in a single query. Certainly, SQL would be quite useless if we were confined to using tables fashioned by other users. One of the language's standout features is our ability to act as both creators and architects of our own data! **In this chapter, we'll delve into our first exploration of how we can create our own tables and integrate information into them, exploring the details of how to create and modify tables' structure.**

5.1. Creating Tables and Insert Information

The first step to create our personalized data in our MySQL **server involves creating a database capable of housing tables relevant to our objectives**. Similar to how "*sakila*" serves as the identifier for our database that contains information about our movie rental store, we must generate a designated "space" where we can subsequently input data.

As has been the case with the majority of SQL commands, creating new databases within MySQL can be executed using a rather straightforward and casual query:

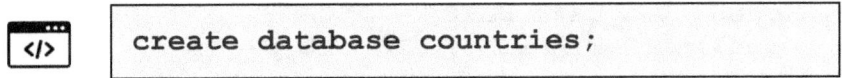
`create database countries;`

The Schemas list on the MySQL menu reveals a change when refreshed (icon on the top right corner), and a new database is now available.

Figure 123 – List of Schemas after creating countries database

In the context of MySQL, the terms "Schemas" and "Databases" are commonly used interchangeably.

This database will serve as the space where we'll construct various tables associated with different countries around the world. We can initiate the process by outlining the structure of our *countries* table. This can be accomplished through the famous "`create table`" command.

But, first.. we define the columns of our table! Our table will contain four:

- *Country ID*: A numerical column serving as the country identifier. This will be an arbitrary number lacking any specific significance.
- *Name*: The name of the country.
- *Foundation Date:* The date when the sovereign state was established.
- *Population*: The country's population quantified in terms of the number of inhabitants.

Creating our table based on the requirements we see above is quite easy:

```
create table countries.countries (
    country_id TINYINT AUTO_INCREMENT PRIMARY KEY,
    name varchar(56) NOT NULL,
    foundation_date DATE,
    population SMALLINT UNSIGNED
);
```

"I want to create a table named countries in the countries schema with 4 columns: country_id, name, foundation_date and population"

The query might seem a bit complex, but we'll simplify it through our usual step-by-step approach:

- Initially, our aim is to establish a table named "*countries*" within the "*countries*" database. This is accomplished using the syntax "`database.table_name`" specifically, "`countries.countries`".

- Following that, we specify that the first column, "*country_id*", should be of type **TINYINT**. Considering that the likelihood of having more than 255 countries to insert into our table is low, **TINYINT** is a nice choice. Additionally, we instruct SQL to automatically increment this column every time a new row is added, and we declare the column as a **PRIMARY KEY**. All these specifications can be included in the same line before the comma.

 PRIMARY KEYS serve as columns ensuring unambiguous identification of each row. Each entry within the column must be distinct and is utilized to uniquely identify each country in our table. In our context, there can't be two country_ids that are equal.

- **The use of a comma helps segment the specifications for different columns**. Following the definition of the "*country_id*" column, we proceed to establish a column named "*name*" configured as a **VARCHAR**, restricted to a maximum of 56 characters, and unable to store **NULL** values. Here, we state that all countries must have a name attached to them.
- Subsequently, we introduce "*foundation_date*" as a column type **DATE**.
- Finally, we designate the "*population*" column in our database table as an integer with the data type **SMALLINT**. It's crucial to note that the range provided by **SMALLINT** may not be sufficient for storing the actual population values. We opt for this data type on purpose to explore and comprehend the implications of breaching constraints within our table.

Upon executing this code block, an interesting development awaits in our schema upon refreshing the MySQL UI:

Figure 124 – Schema Information

103

Expanding the arrow next to the *countries* table reveals additional details about the existing columns, specifically the ones we've recently established. If the table appears to be created, does it currently hold any data?

Let's investigate with the usual `SELECT` command:

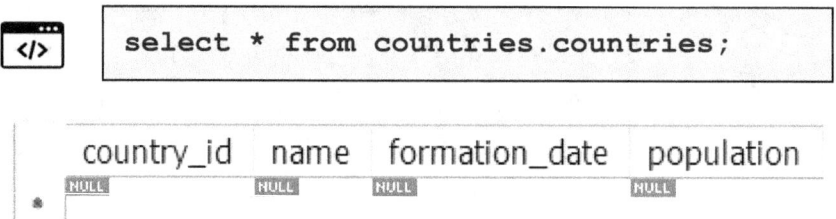

Figure 125 – countries table

It's empty, of course! The takeaway: when employing the `CREATE TABLE` command to generate tables, we establish empty tables void of data. While our table has the structure we've outlined (primarily in terms of column names), it lacks any actual rows. Of course, the subsequent course of action involves populating our countries table with data. For this task, we'll employ the well-known `INSERT INTO` command:

```
insert into countries.countries (
    name, foundation_date, population
) values (
    'Portugal',
    '1143-10-05',
    10154934
);
```

"I want to insert a row with values Portugal, '1143-10-05' and 1015493 in the name, foundation_date and population columns in the countries.countries table"

In this code, we are using the `insert into` command to insert data into our table `countries.countries`. First, we provide the columns where we want to insert data inside the parenthesis and then we provide the data we want to insert in the same order.

In the code above, we are:

- Inserting **Portugal** into the **name** column.
- Inserting '1143-10-05' into the **foundation_date** column.
- Inserting **10154934** into the **population** column.

Notice that we are not providing any value to the **country_id** column – we will see why in a minute. Also, after trying to insert data, we'll have an error! Why?

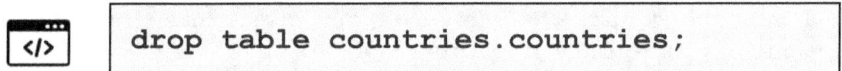

Figure 126 – Error on Inserting Data into Population

The problem is that we are attempting to insert an integer value into the "**population**" column and the value we are inserting exceeds the allowable range of the **SMALLINT** data type. The **SMALLINT** type only accommodates integers up to 32.767, and since we're trying to insert the value 10 million, SQL encounters an inconsistency and cannot proceed with the insertion.

To address this, we have to make a structural change to the table to rectify this behavior. Let's do it in the most non-productive way possible, by deleting and creating the table again. Initially, we'll remove the existing table using the **DROP** command:

```
drop table countries.countries;
```

Note: If the code above does not work in your environment, run this code first: **SET SQL_SAFE_UPDATES = 0;**

After dropping the table, we can recreate it again, but this time we will change the integer data type we were providing in the **population** column to **INT**.

```
create table countries.countries (
    country_id TINYINT AUTO_INCREMENT PRIMARY KEY,
    name varchar(56) NOT NULL,
    foundation_date DATE,
    population INT UNSIGNED
);
```

The **INT** data type conveniently accommodates integer values up to 2.147.483.647, providing ample capacity for our data requirements!

Now, let's proceed with attempting to insert data into our table once again:

```
insert into countries.countries (
    name, foundation_date, population
) values (
    'Portugal',
    '1143-10-05',
    10154934
);
```

No error, cool! And now, let's confirm that the data was inserted using **SELECT ***:

country_id	name	foundation_date	population
1	Portugal	1143-10-05	10154934

Figure 127 – countries table with 1 row inserted

Let's pause for a moment to mark the success of our initial insert operation. It's indeed a noteworthy milestone in your journey of learning SQL!

After executing the above code, you might be left with some questions. For example, why aren't we specifying the `country_id`, and why does the table show the value 1 being inserted? This is because we've indicated that the column `country_id` should automatically increment within the table, a feature linked to the **AUTO INCREMENT** property we've employed. Each time a new row is added to the table, a new `country_id` is assigned based on the last available `country_id`. Following this logic, the next row inserted in this table will have `country_id = 2`.

It's also worth mentioning that we can insert data into specific columns. The only restriction in the **INSERT INTO** is that we must provide data for all columns marked as **NOT NULL** or those serving as a primary key for the table. Let's try to insert another row into the countries table by providing information about France but this time skipping the information about the `foundation_date`.

```
insert into countries.countries (
    name, population
) values (
    'France',
    65476395
);
```

country_id	name	foundation_date	population
1	Portugal	1143-10-05	10154934
2	France	NULL	65476395

Figure 128 – countries table with 2 rows inserted

When we skip a column in the **INSERT INTO** statement, it will be added as **NULL** value in the output. We've just created our first **missing value** [24]!

Another cool thing: we are not restricted to a single row when inserting data. We can also insert multiple rows very easily using the following syntax:

```
insert into countries.countries (
    name, population
) values ('Spain', 46780219),
('Canada', 38205830);
```

Checking our countries table again:

country_id	name	foundation_date	population
1	Portugal	1143-10-05	10154934
2	France	NULL	65476395
3	Spain	NULL	46780219
4	Canada	NULL	38205830

Figure 129 – countries table with 4 rows inserted

---

[24] Remember that missing values are values that represent "emptiness" or "non-existent"

107

Two rows were added at the same time! By using commas to separate the different rows that we want to insert, they could both be added simultaneously.

Continuing to explore our **CREATE TABLE** properties. remember the **UNSIGNED** attribute we've defined in the **CREATE TABLE** statement? If you don't, I've got your back – here's the code again.

```
create table countries.countries (
    country_id TINYINT AUTO_INCREMENT PRIMARY KEY,
    name varchar(56) NOT NULL,
    foundation_date DATE,
    population INT UNSIGNED
);
```

The **UNSIGNED** property prevents adding negative values to an integer column. As we are pretty rebel, let's try to insert negative population values into the *countries.countries* table:

```
insert into countries.countries (
    name, population
) values ('United Kingdom', -1000);
```

The code will trigger an "out of range" error when executed, since inserting negative values into **UNSIGNED** integers is not allowed, as seen in Figure 130.

Message
Error Code: 1264. Out of range value for column 'population' at row 1

Figure 130 – Out of range error with unsigned property

Ok, now is the time for you to do some experiments by inserting various types of data into our table! Experiment across different columns and check patterns across different data types, this should give you a good overview on the restrictions we have created with our defined data types.

Let me try some more examples with you – starting by trying to insert plain text into the *population* column:

```
insert into countries.countries (
    name, population
) values ('United Kingdom', 'ABC');
```

We have another error! This time, the error message states: *incorrect integer value error*.

Message
Error Code: 1366. Incorrect integer value: 'ABC' for column 'population' at row 1

Figure 131 – Incorrect integer Value error

This error states that inserting plain text into this column is not allowed, as we expect. This reinforces the idea that the data types we use entirely dictate the kind of data that our columns can accommodate.

Continuing with more experiments: let's use another **CREATE TABLE** command to create a new table:

```
create table countries.codes (
    country_code varchar(3) NOT NULL
);
```

Can you identify the table we've created just by looking at the **CREATE TABLE** command?

With the query above, we have created an empty table called *countries.codes* with just a single column:

country_code

Figure 132 – countries.codes table

Notice that our column is only able to hold 3 characters. This is defined by the data type **VARCHAR(3)**. First, let's try to insert a row that respects this condition:

```
insert into countries.codes (
    country_code
) values ('PRT');
```

Cool - all clear and no error, as we can see in Figure 133.

	country_code
▶	PRT

Figure 133 – countries.codes table with 1 row

But what if we try to insert a row with 4 characters? Let'see:

```
insert into countries.codes (
    country_code
) values ('FRAN');
```

Message
Error Code: 1406. Data too long for column 'country_code' at row 1

Figure 134 – Text Overflow error

As expected, we have an error with this **INSERT INTO** command! This arises from the limitation of our table's *country_code* column, that is unable to accommodate text with a length over 3 characters. And.. what happens if we try to insert an integer into this table?

```
insert into countries.codes (
    country_code
) values (123);
```

In this scenario, SQL automatically converts the data. While it can successfully insert 123 into the table, it will be added as a character data type. You can verify this by describing the `countries.codes` table after performing the insert operation and see that the column remains `VARCHAR(3)`:

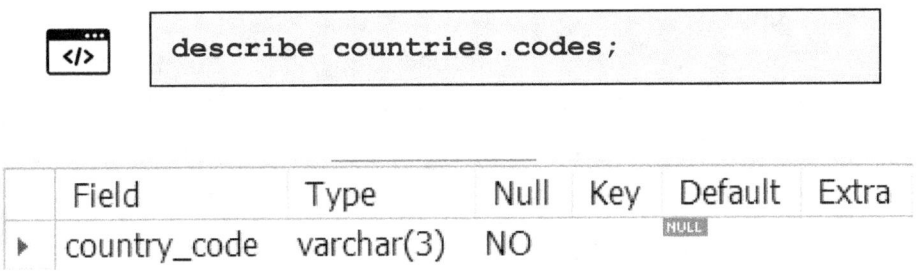

Figure 135 – Describing countries.codes table

Despite MySQL converting the value, it doesn't change the column data type in any manner!

In wrapping up this chapter on creating tables and inserting data into our MySQL database, we've laid down the foundation for two of the most important skills on our data journey. With the `CREATE TABLE` and `INSERT INTO` commands, we've taken the first steps towards giving life to our database. From defining column structures to navigating data types and constraints, we've learned to wield SQL tools with precision. **As we've delved into the realms of creating tables and populating them with data, it's essential to recognize that database management involves not only the addition but also the removal of data.** Just as we've learned to construct and insert data into tables, the next logical step in our journey is to understand the process of deleting data. So, in the upcoming chapter, we will explore the mechanisms and commands necessary to remove data from our tables effectively.

5.2. Deleting Data and Dropping Tables

For this chapter, let's use the `countries` table that contains the following data:

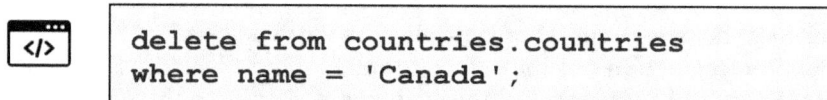

Figure 136 – countries.countries table

Note: *If you don't have this table created in your environment, use the CREATE TABLE and INSERT INTO commands we've just learned before.*

A frequent task in managing data involves the need to eliminate specific rows from a table. For example, imagine a scenario where we aim to remove the entry corresponding to "*Canada*" in the table depicted in Figure 136. This task can be accomplished through the use of a new clause **DELETE FROM** statement (coupled with the familiar **WHERE** clause):

```
delete from countries.countries
where name = 'Canada';
```

Here, we're removing all rows from the table where the "*name*" column equals "*Canada*". The **DELETE FROM** states the intention of deleting an element from the table, while the **WHERE** clause filters the rows we intend to delete. But when attempting to execute the code mentioned, you might encounter an unusual error in MySQL:

#	Time	Acti	Message
⊗	1 19:23:57	d...	Error Code: 1175. You are using safe update mode and you tried to update a table without a WHERE that uses a KEY column.

Figure 137 – Error when deleting rows

This is something specific of MySQL WorkBench and Server. MySQL has a built-in safeguard that prevents the deletion of records when the **DELETE FROM** command is used. This safety measure, known as safe update mode, restricts the execution of delete statements until the option is disabled. The rationale behind this approach is to mitigate the risk of unintentional deletions or drops in our database server, especially in production databases where such actions could have significant consequences. To deactivate this option, you can use the user interface or execute the following SQL statement in your script:

```
SET SQL_SAFE_UPDATES = 0;
```

After running this command, we can now execute the **DELETE FROM** statement with success:

```
delete from countries.countries
where name = 'Canada';
```

> "I want to delete all rows from the countries.countries table where the name of the country is Canada".

This will carry out a *delete statement*, eliminating the row for the country named '*Canada*' from the *countries.countries* table. After removing the row and upon selecting all rows from the table, the results will now display as follows:

country_id	name	foundation_date	population
1	Portugal	1143-10-05	10154934
2	France	NULL	65476395
3	Spain	NULL	46780219

Figure 138 – countries.countries table after deleting Canada row

We now only have three countries left in the table as the **DELETE FROM** command removed all rows that met the conditions specified in the **WHERE** clause of the query. The interesting part? All the filtering concepts we've covered apply when it comes to deleting data!

We've covered how to delete rows - but is it possible to delete entire tables? Absolutely, and it's quite straightforward with the famous **DROP TABLE** command:

```
DROP TABLE countries.countries;
```

We need to be very careful when working with DELETE FROM and DROP TABLE commands. These are likely the types of commands that have caused more issues in production databases.

The drop table command completely wipes out the table from the database so be very cautious when using it. Let's visualize the tables available in the countries database after executing this destructive command:

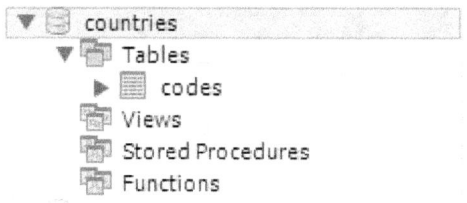

Figure 139 – countries schema after deleting our countries.countries table.

The **countries** table is gone! We can also confirm this by trying to run the select statement that we've done in the beginning of this chapter:

```
select * from countries.countries;
```

We'll have an error upon executing this statement, similar to the one depicted in Figure 140.

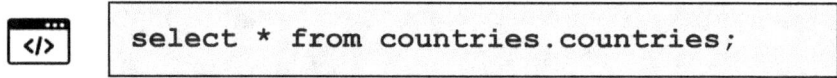

Figure 140 – Error when querying countries.countries after deleting the table.

As this table no longer exists in the countries database, we can't really reference it on any SQL statement.

In this chapter, we delved into the crucial aspects of managing data within tables, focusing on the **DELETE** and **DROP TABLE** commands in MySQL. With these commands, we've gained essential skills in manipulating data within tables, ensuring both precision and prudence in our database management practices. In the following chapters, we'll continue to expand our knowledge, exploring more advanced SQL functionalities to further enhance our data management capabilities, particularly how to change and delete columns.

5.3. Deleting Columns and Altering Tables

For this chapter, we'll need to recreate the *countries.countries* table again. If you have deleted the table in the preceding chapter, you can create the table again by running the code below. The provided code creates the "*countries.countries*" table and inserts a single row containing information about Portugal:

```
create table countries.countries (
    country_id TINYINT AUTO_INCREMENT PRIMARY KEY,
    name varchar(56) NOT NULL,
    foundation_date DATE,
    population INT UNSIGNED
);

insert into countries.countries (
    name, foundation_date, population
) values (
    'Portugal',
    '1143-10-05',
    10154934
);
```

So far, we've explored the method of removing rows from SQL tables using the combination of **DELETE FROM** and the **WHERE** clause. Can we apply a similar approach to delete columns? Unfortunately no, and we need to physically change the structure of the table with a new command: **ALTER TABLE**!

Let's explore it in the code below:

```
ALTER TABLE countries.countries
    DROP COLUMN foundation_date;
```

Take note: the **ALTER TABLE** command is extremely important! It empowers us to make concrete changes to the undelying table structure, something that we haven't been able until now! **This marks the first time in our learning journey where we can modify the underlying tables' structure, going beyond mere result output.** In this example, we use **ALTER TABLE** and **DROP COLUMN** command, eliminating the specific column named in the latter.

A SELECT statement consistently generates a new "object" known as a set, without altering the table directly. Conversely, ALTER TABLE and INSERT INTO operate directly on the tables, causing immediate changes to the data or table structure.

After executing the given command, an interesting observation emerges: there isn't any output! This is similar to how an "**INSERT INTO**" operation behaves, altering data within the table without presenting a visible result – the difference is that **ALTER TABLE** changes the table structure in somw way. When we now query *countries.countries* table again, a new aspect comes to light:

country_id	name	population
1	Portugal	10154934
NULL	NULL	NULL

Figure 141– Querying countries.countries after deleting the column.

In this new version of the *countries.countries* table, the **foundation_date** column doesn't exist anymore! **ALTER TABLE** is then able to introduce new functionalities as we can now make modifications to the table structures. The power of **ALTER TABLE** is huge: it enables us to perform various tasks, ranging from renaming column names to changing data types.

For example, let's start to investigate that by checking the current state of the columns of the *countries.countries* table:

```
DESCRIBE countries.countries;
```

Field	Type	Null	Key	Default	Extra
country_id	tinyint	NO	PRI	NULL	auto_increment
name	varchar(56)	NO		NULL	
population	int unsigned	YES		NULL	

Figure 142– Describing countries.countries table

As you already know how the **DESCRIBE** output works, can you guess what's the data type of the *population* column?

...

It's an **int**!

Now, suppose we want to conserve some memory space on our computer and convert the population column to a **smallint** data type. Is that even possible? Yes, as we can use the **ALTER TABLE** command combined with the **MODIFY** clause to adjust column types:

```
ALTER TABLE countries.countries
    MODIFY population SMALLINT;
```

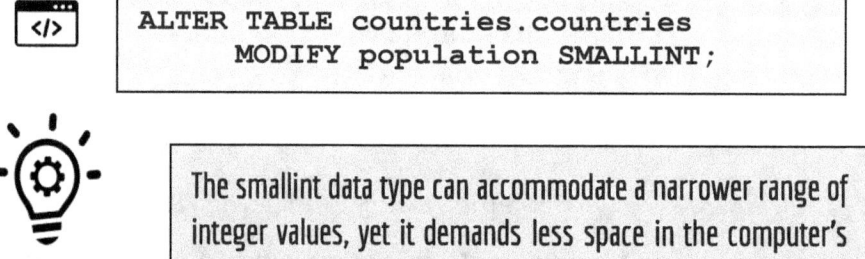

The smallint data type can accommodate a narrower range of integer values, yet it demands less space in the computer's memory.

Unfortunately, this code will not work! Why? (I think you already know the answer!)

But basically, it's due to the presence of values in those columns that exceed the **smallint** capacity! Upon executing the provided code, the error in Figure 143 appears.

Message
Error Code: 1264. Out of range value for column 'population' at row 1

Figure 143– Overflowing population's smallint

You probably already know this rule.. we must comply with everything we know about data types for our **ALTER TABLE** commands to work! This is very similar to every operation we've used in SQL until now.

Given that, do you think that we can change our column to a **BIGINT** data type? Let's see:

```
ALTER TABLE countries.countries
    MODIFY population BIGINT;
```

In this case, the column is changed successfully! As the data type we are trying to change to is valid for all the values that the column contains at the moment, the SQL command ran succesfully. Let's confirm that our columns was changed with the **DESCRIBE** command:

```
DESCRIBE countries.countries;
```

Field	Type	Null	Key	Default	Extra
country_id	tinyint	NO	PRI	NULL	auto_increment
name	varchar(56)	NO		NULL	
population	bigint	YES		NULL	

Figure 144 – Describing countries.countries table after changing the column data type

Voilá! Our column has been successfully modified, and we now boast a new datatype in our *countries* table. Take note that this specific concern related to data types might happen with **VARCHAR** columns as well. For example, let's try to reduce the length of the **'country name'** field, presently collapsing to a length of 4 characters.

```
ALTER TABLE countries.countries
    MODIFY name varchar(4);
```

An error will pop up:

Message
Error Code: 1265. Data truncated for column 'name' at row 1

Figure 145– Error on Changing VARCHAR column in countries table

However, can you anticipate the outcome if we adjust our column size to accommodate 60 characters? Let's find out:

```
ALTER TABLE countries.countries
    MODIFY name varchar(60);
```

This will work just fine and the data types for our table will be successfully modified!

Field	Type	Null	Key	Default	Extra
country_id	tinyint	NO	PRI	NULL	auto_increment
name	varchar(60)	YES		NULL	
population	bigint	YES		NULL	

Figure 146– Successfully Changing our Countries table

Awesome!

As we conclude this chapter on creating tables and manipulating data within MySQL databases, we find ourselves armed with foundational skills that are key in our journey of mastering SQL. Through the **CREATE TABLE** and **INSERT INTO** commands, we've laid the groundwork for bringing life into our databases. Alongside this, we've delved into the detail of managing data, from understanding data types and constraints to the nuances of inserting, updating, and deleting data. Our exploration has gone through the power of SQL commands like **DELETE FROM** and **DROP TABLE**, allowing us to fit our databases to suit our needs. Moreover, we've embraced the transformative potential of the **ALTER TABLE** command, empowering us to evolve the very structure of our tables. As we venture forward, we set our sights on further refining our mastery of SQL, let's practice these concepts related to manipulating the structure and data of the tables.

5.4. Exercise Section

As always, in this coding exercise section, you'll have the opportunity to apply what we've learned. This time, we'll hone your skills in modifying and changing tables. Let's start by running a script that will generate the table required for querying in this exercise section:

```
CREATE TABLE exercises.customers (
    customer_id integer,
    customer_name varchar(30),
    customer_age integer,
    birth_date varchar(10),
    country_code varchar(4));
```

If this code executed correctly, continue to 5.4.1. If not, you may have encountered a "database doesn't exist" error. This happens because you haven't executed the code in Exercise Section 3.5. To ensure the code above functions properly, execute the command: "**CREATE DATABASE exercises;**" and then try to run the code once more.

5.4.1. Exercises

1. Insert two customers into the *customers* table:

- Customer ID 1, "John" with 25 years old that was born on the 1st of September of 1991 and has a country code of "123".

- Customer ID 2, "Anne" with 45 years old that was born on the 4th of October of 1975 and has a country code of "324".

2. Insert a new customer into the *customers* table:

- Customer ID 3, "Joseph" that has a country code of "123". The other variables are unknown.

3. Delete all the customers from the customers table with *country_code* = '123'

4. Delete all the customers from the customers table with *country_code* = '324' OR that are less than 26 years old.

5. Delete the *birth_date* column from the customers table

5.4.2. Exercise Solutions

```
1. INSERT INTO exercises.customers_validation (
    customer_id, customer_name, customer_age, birth_date, country_code
)VALUES (1, "John", 25, '1991-09-01', "123"),
       (2, "Anne", 45, '1975-10-04', "324");

2. INSERT INTO exercises.customers (
    customer_id, customer_name, country_code
)VALUES (3, "Joseph", "123");

3. DELETE FROM exercises.customers
WHERE country_code = "123";

4. DELETE FROM exercises.customers
WHERE country_code = "324" OR customer_age <26;

5. ALTER TABLE exercises.customers
    DROP COLUMN birth_date;
```

6. Combining Tables

In SQL, it's uncommon to work solely with standalone tables without establishing connections between them. This highlights one of the potential challenges for beginners when navigating the language. In this section, we'll mainly learn two important concepts that developers often employ to combine different tables:

- Utilizing table joins to merge distinct domains and retrieve additional columns;
- Employing union operators to vertically stack tables;

6.1. Inner Join

Let's revisit the *sakila* database, this time focusing on the *rental* table, which holds details regarding customer rentals.

```
SELECT rental_id, customer_id FROM
sakila.rental;
```

rental_id	customer_id
76	1
573	1
1185	1
1422	1
1476	1
1725	1

Figure 147– Rental_id and customer_id columns from the rental table

Consider a scenario where we aim to incorporate customer names into this table by referencing each customer's *customer_id*. For instance, we know that the customer names can be retrieved from the *sakila.customer* table, as illustrated in Figure 148.

123

	customer_id	first_name	last_name
▶	1	MARY	SMITH
	2	PATRICIA	JOHNSON
	3	LINDA	WILLIAMS
	4	BARBARA	JONES
	5	ELIZABETH	BROWN
	6	JENNIFER	DAVIS
	7	MARIA	MILLER

Figure 148 – sakila.customer table

To integrate customers' first names and last names into the data depicted in Figure 147, we need to understand the concept of **SQL Join**. Joining is a fundamental concept in the realm of databases, albeit one that many find challenging to grasp. This operation enables us to merge data from different tables, adding to the available information in a highly beneficial manner.

First, let's see the **JOIN** syntax using MySQL:

```
select rental.rental_id, rental.customer_id,
cust.first_name, cust.last_name
from sakila.rental as rental
inner join sakila.customer as cust
on rental.customer_id = cust.customer_id;
```

As this query is a bit complex, it will be useful to translate it into natural language:

"I aim to retrieve the rental_id and customer_id from the sakila.rental table. Additionally, I intend to obtain the first_name and last_name from the customer table. To establish a connection between the two tables, I will use customer_id."

rental_id	customer_id	first_name	last_name
76	1	MARY	SMITH
573	1	MARY	SMITH
1185	1	MARY	SMITH
1422	1	MARY	SMITH
1476	1	MARY	SMITH
1725	1	MARY	SMITH
2308	1	MARY	SMITH

Figure 149 – Joined Data Result

At first glance, the syntax for SQL JOINs might seem complex, but as you become more familiar with it, you'll find it surprisingly intuitive and easy to figure out the columns and join conditions to employ. Our query begins by pinpointing the exact columns required for our query, making use of the famous **SELECT** statement:

```
select rental.rental_id, rental.customer_id,
       cust.first_name, cust.last_name
```

Notice the introduction of a new element in this context: the use of two distinct aliases preceding the column names, namely *'rental'* and *'cust'*. These aliases serve as pointers, guiding the join operation on the specific columns to select from various tables. **While table aliases may not have significantly improved our operations with individual tables, their usefulness becomes particularly evident when working with joins, providing clarity and the ability to read our queries.**

Let's consider the next part of our query, where we provide the table information:

```
from sakila.rental as rental
inner join sakila.customer as cust
```

This is the stage where we assign aliases to our tables. For instance, `'sakila.rental'` will be referred to as `'rental'` and `'sakila.customer'` will be known as `'cust'` throughout the query. This will help SQL map the relevant columns from the correct tables. And, finally, we must inform SQL about the specific column to use for connecting our tables. This can be achieved by adding an **ON** clause to our query:

```
on rental.customer_id = cust.customer_id;
```

In this context, we are indicating our intention to match all **customer_id** entries in the left table with those in the right table. The terms "left" and "right" become clearer when we visualize them in the diagram on Figure 150.

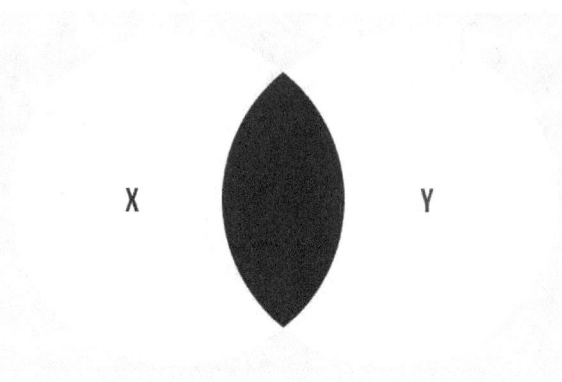

Figure 150 – Venn Diagram of an Inner Join

X and Y tables are placeholder names that you may find when speaking about SQL Joins in other resources. If we name table X as the "left table" and table Y as the "right table," our join can be illustrated as Figure 150 states. In an inner join, we instruct SQL to retrieve all rows where the connecting column (key) is found in both tables. **The linkage will take place between each customer_id in the rental table (left, X table) with every matching customer_id in the cust table (right, Y table).**

Let's use customer_id 1 as an example, which represents "*Mary Smith*". SQL will look for the matching *customer_id* in the *sakila.customer* table and retrieve the *first_name* and *last_name* values linked with customer_id 1.

rental_id	customer_id	first_name	last_name
76	1	MARY	SMITH
573	1	MARY	SMITH
1185	1	MARY	SMITH
1422	1	MARY	SMITH
1476	1	MARY	SMITH
1725	1	MARY	SMITH
2308	1	MARY	SMITH

Figure 151 – Customer ID 1 (data returned from join)

The identical mapping is employed for all other *customer_ids* found in both tables. And did you notice the **INNER JOIN** keyword? That term determines the **type of join** we're doing.

We've used this keyword as we aim to include only the rows where the key is present in both tables. **If a *customer_id* exists solely in either the rentals or customer tables, that customer won't be included in the resulting set.** Apart from the inner join, there are also other well-known joins, such as the Left and Right Joins.

We'll also illustrate them here! To do it more effectively, let's generate some new tables that will assist us in the next part of this chapter.

```sql
CREATE DATABASE SANDBOX;

CREATE TABLE sandbox.customers(
    customer_id INT AUTO_INCREMENT PRIMARY KEY,
    customer_name varchar(255) NOT NULL
);

CREATE TABLE sandbox.customer_country(
    customer_id INT PRIMARY KEY,
    customer_country varchar(255) NOT NULL
);

insert into sandbox.customers (
    customer_name
) values ('John'), ('Adam'), ('Anne'), ('May'),
('Susan'), ('Joe');

insert into sandbox.customer_country (
    customer_id, customer_country
) values (1, 'USA'), (3, 'USA'), (4, 'UK'), (5, 'UK'),
(7, 'UK');
```

For our upcoming explanation, we will create a new multi-purpose database called *'sandbox'*. This database will house broader and more generic examples of data that we will create manually. It will expose us to diverse types of data and various table structures not related with the *sakila* database.

In these two tables that we've just created, we will store information about fictional customers and their respective country. Let's first investigate both tables with the usual suspect – the **SELECT** statement.

```
SELECT * FROM sandbox.customers;
```

customer_id	customer_name
1	John
2	Adam
3	Anne
4	May
5	Susan
6	Joe

Figure 152 – sandbox.customers table

This simple table holds details about fictional customer IDs and names. We've added six distinct customers, each with a unique name. On the other hand, the *customer_country* table includes data about some of these customers and the countries they hail from:

customer_id	customer_country
1	USA
3	USA
4	UK
5	UK
7	UK

Figure 153 – sandbox.customer_country table

The `customer_id` found in the *customer_country* table corresponds to the same customer in the *customer* table. For instance, customer_id 1 belongs to John from the USA. Regarding this match between both tables, two notable points emerge:

- We lack country information for *Adam* and *Joe*.
- There is no data available about the name of customer id 7, a customer from the UK.

This missing information will be crucial for grasping the concepts of left and right joins. Let's consider, for a moment, that we assume a scenario were only `INNER JOIN`s are available in the language:

```
select cust.customer_id, cust.customer_name,
country.customer_country
from sandbox.customers as cust
inner join sandbox.customer_country as country
on cust.customer_id = country.customer_id;
```

Recall that an inner join performs the following operation:

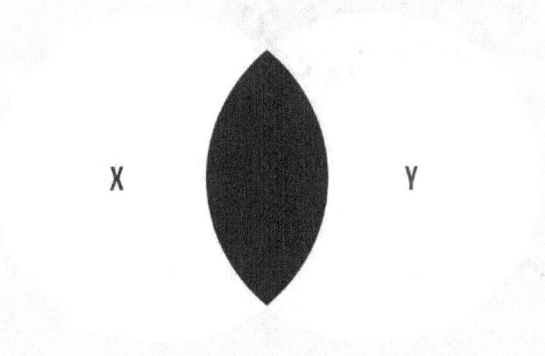

Figure 154 – inner join diagram

As we've seen before, only the shaded "domain" will be included in the resulting table. Now, let's see the consequences of applying this inner join to our "*customer*" example:

customer_id	customer_name	customer_country
1	John	USA
3	Anne	USA
4	May	UK
5	Susan	UK

Figure 155 – inner join example on our customer and customer country examples

The output only consists of the *customer_ids* found in both tables! Any other information is lost during the joining process, particularly information for customers that show up in only one of the tables. This is where understanding the syntax for **LEFT** and **RIGHT** joins comes in handy.

To illustrate, let's see a diagram of a left join first. It notably encompasses a different domain that the **INNER**, as shown in the following figure:

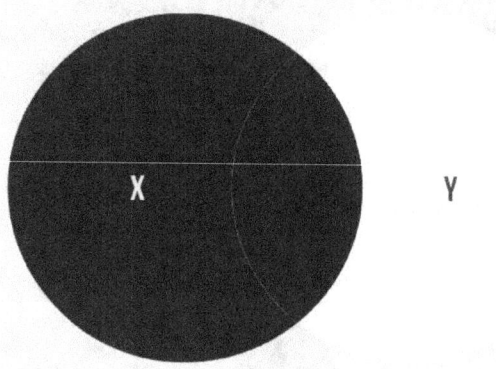

Figure 156 – Left Join diagram

How can we perform a **LEFT** join in SQL? As we continue to navigate the details of SQL, remember that while the syntax may seem daunting at first, with practice and perseverance, it becomes very easy to understand and work it. Luckily, the syntax for **LEFT** and **RIGHT** joins is not much different from the **INNER JOIN** one.

As we progress through the book, these differences become particularly significant as we come across situations where there could be missing information in one of the tables being joined. When dealing with actual data from companies and organizations, this situation arises frequently, and understanding which JOIN to utilize becomes essential for effectively managing the data within them.

6.2 Left and Right Join

To perform a **LEFT** or **RIGHT** join we only have to switch the keyword in the join clause, namely replacing **INNER**. For example:

```
select cust.customer_id, cust.customer_name,
country.customer_country
from sandbox.customers as cust
left join sandbox.customer_country as country
on cust.customer_id = country.customer_id;
```

A left join ensures that every data from the table on the left (preceding the left keyword) is included in the resulting set. Also, any available information from the right table that corresponds to the common keys will be present as well. So, what sets left join apart from an inner join is its ability to retain elements that may be absent in the right table, showing those attributes as **NULL**.

customer_id	customer_name	customer_country
1	John	USA
2	Adam	NULL
3	Anne	USA
4	May	UK
5	Susan	UK
6	Joe	NULL

Figure 157 – Left Join Output

Currently, our output features six customers from the *customers* table. However, there's a catch - the *customer_country* field will display as **NULL** for customers whose country information is unavailable. This situation shows up when SQL cannot find a corresponding value for certain customer_ids in the *customer_country* table.

Based on these two tables and the ideas we know about left joins, can you anticipate the output of a right join? Let's find out!

```
select cust.customer_id, cust.customer_name,
country.customer_country
from sandbox.customers as cust
right join sandbox.customer_country as country
on cust.customer_id = country.customer_id;
```

customer_id	customer_name	customer_country
1	John	USA
3	Anne	USA
4	May	UK
5	Susan	UK
NULL	NULL	UK

Figure 158 – Right Join Output

The diagram of a "Right Join" domain is the following:

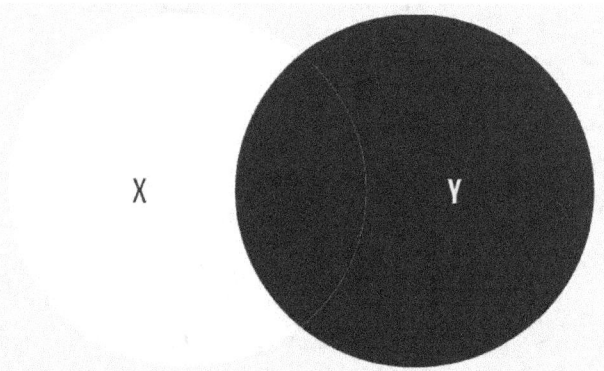

Figure 159 – Right Join Diagram

An unusual outcome is that we have 5 rows in the table, yet there are only 4 customers with a valid *customer_id*. This anomaly occurs as we extract the *customer_id* column from the left table, and even though the column is present in both tables, we are referencing the *customer_id* from the *country* table. If we want to obtain all *customer_ids*, we need to adjust our query to reference the key from the "main table" in the join.

```
select country.customer_id, cust.customer_name,
country.customer_country
from sandbox.customers as cust
right join sandbox.customer_country as country
on cust.customer_id = country.customer_id;
```

customer_id	customer_name	customer_country
1	John	USA
3	Anne	USA
4	May	UK
5	Susan	UK
7	NULL	UK

Figure 160 – Right Join Output

In the last query, we made adjustments to the aliases in the **SELECT** statement. Instead of employing "`select cust.customer_id`", we opted for "`select country.customer_id`". Remember: **in left or right joins, it's advisable to select the column key from the table that commands the join.**

In Left and Right joins, you normally select the column key from the commanding table on the join.

In this context, what does "commanding table" mean? In a left join, it refers to the table mentioned first (in the diagram, *table x*), while in a right join, the commanding table is the one mentioned after the **JOIN** statement (in the diagram, table *y*). So, the output in Figure 160 aligns with the understanding we've developed about joins. In the resulting output, we notice that *customer_name* is **NULL** for customer 7, indicating a lack of information about this customer's name in the *sandbox.customers* table. If you would like to practice joins a bit more, there are other tables in the *sakila* database that contain ids that can be used to create links between tables! Can you find them and practice these **JOIN** operations?

I understand that the concept of joins can seem daunting initially. Typically, it takes considerable practice to fully comprehend and excel in using them. However, I hope this explanation serves as a solid introduction to connecting different tables within the realm of SQL.

Thus far, we can all acknowledge that joins offer great flexibility. We've covered inner, left, and right joins, but did you know that we can further expand the utilization of key columns? For instance, we can employ multiple columns in the join key. Multi-key joins entail the use of multiple columns as keys for linking tables, enabling more intricate relationships and data integration. The upcoming chapter will delve into the intricacies of executing them, exploring their applications, and highlighting their advantages in database queries.

6.3 Multi-key Joins

Multiple key joins, a prevalent practice in SQL, involve combining data from two or more tables based on multiple matching columns. This method facilitates the integration of datasets with complex relationships **by establishing connections through several shared attributes**. By leveraging these multi-column associations, SQL queries can retrieve precise and comprehensive results, enhancing the flexibility and depth of data analysis and manipulation.

To exemplify multiple key joins, we are going to create two new tables:

- *customer_month*, that has a registry of each customer per month on a fictional store. The table contains *customer_id, month* and *customer_name*.

- *customer_balance*, a table that stores data regarding each customer's financial balance over various months.

```sql
CREATE TABLE sandbox.customer_month(
    customer_id INT,
    month INT,
    customer_name varchar(255) NOT NULL,
    PRIMARY KEY (customer_id, month)
);

CREATE TABLE sandbox.customer_balance(
    customer_id INT,
    month INT,
    balance numeric(10,2),
    PRIMARY KEY (customer_id, month)
);

insert into sandbox.customer_month (
    customer_id, month, customer_name
) values (1, 201903, 'John'), (1, 201904, 'John'), (1, 201905, 'John'),
(2, 201903, 'May'), (2, 201904, 'May'), (2, 201905, 'May'), (2, 201906, 'May');

insert into sandbox.customer_balance (
    customer_id, month, balance
) values (1, 201903, 10.00), (1, 201904, 15.00),
 (2, 201903, 1524.00), (2, 201904, 225.00), (3, 201905, 360.00);
```

Let's first preview this pair of tables with some **SELECT** statements:

customer_id	month	customer_name
1	201903	John
1	201904	John
1	201905	John
2	201903	May
2	201904	May
2	201905	May
2	201906	May

Figure 161 – Preview of customer_month

The *customer_month* table displays several rows for each customer, varying based on the interactions they've had with our company. For instance, John engaged with our company in March, April, and May, whereas customer May interacted with us in March, April, May, and June.

Now, let's examine the *customer_balance* table:

customer_id	month	balance
1	201903	10.00
1	201904	15.00
2	201903	1524.00
2	201904	225.00
3	201905	360.00

Figure 162 – Preview of customer_balance

This table provides the customer balance for each customer in a particular month. In the given example, *customer_id* 1 (identified as John in the *customer_month* table) had balances of 10 and 15 dollars in March and April.

If we aim to combine these two tables, what column should we employ as the key for the join? Let's attempt to only use the *customer_id* column and perform an inner join, which will only merge customers present in both tables.

```
SELECT a.customer_id, a.customer_name, b.month, b.balance
FROM sandbox.customer_month as a
INNER JOIN sandbox.customer_balance as b
ON a.customer_id = b.customer_id;
```

customer_id	customer_name	month	balance
1	John	201903	10.00
1	John	201903	10.00
1	John	201903	10.00
1	John	201904	15.00
1	John	201904	15.00
1	John	201904	15.00
2	May	201903	1524.00
2	May	201903	1524.00
2	May	201903	1524.00
2	May	201903	1524.00
2	May	201904	225.00
2	May	201904	225.00
2	May	201904	225.00

Figure 163 – Combining customer_balance and customer_month using customer_id

Something has certainly gone wrong! It's worth noting that we seem to be tripling the customer balances (which our customers might not mind, for sure!). How did this happen? In essence, as we have seen, a join operation functions by identifying and matching up any common keys present in two tables. There are three occurrences of *customer_id* 1 in table a (customer_month) and two occurrences in table b (*customer_balance*). As a result of the join operation, six rows will be generated for this customer, as this is the multiplication of the rows we have on each side of the join.

However, this outcome seems incorrect as we shouldn't be multiplying the balances of customers in a given month by three. The error becomes even more apparent when we incorporate the months from both tables into the output. In the next query, we'd like to observe both *a.month* and *b.month, customer_month* and *customer_balance* respectively:

```
select a.customer_id, a.customer_name, a.month, b.month,
b.balance
from sandbox.customer_month as a
inner join sandbox.customer_balance as b
on a.customer_id = b.customer_id;
```

customer_id	customer_name	month	month	balance
1	John	201903	201903	10.00
1	John	201904	201903	10.00
1	John	201905	201903	10.00
1	John	201903	201904	15.00
1	John	201904	201904	15.00
1	John	201905	201904	15.00
2	May	201903	201903	1524.00
2	May	201904	201903	1524.00
2	May	201905	201903	1524.00
2	May	201906	201903	1524.00
2	May	201903	201904	225.00
2	May	201904	201904	225.00
2	May	201905	201904	225.00
2	May	201906	201904	225.00

Figure 164 – Combining customer_balance and customer_month using customer_id

Now this is interesting. Notice that the initial column labeled `'month'` sources its data from *'customer_balance'*, while the second column derives its data from *'customer_month'*. It seems that our months are getting mixed up in the output table. To go around the issue of duplicate rows - a very common mistake often made during SQL programming - **we should utilize a multiple key join.**

This is a task that can be achieved by using the '**AND**' keyword in our join on the '**ON**' clause – in our example, we want to combine the data by *customer_id* AND by *month*.

```
select a.customer_id, a.customer_name, b.month, b.balance
from sandbox.customer_month as a
inner join sandbox.customer_balance as b
on a.customer_id = b.customer_id and
a.month = b.month;
```

customer_id	customer_name	month	balance
1	John	201903	10.00
1	John	201904	15.00
2	May	201903	1524.00
2	May	201904	225.00

Figure 165 – Using a multi-key Join

Now, SQL isn't just searching for the identical *customer_id* in the b table but is also seeking the combination of *customer_id* + *month*, establishing the relationship we aimed for. Understanding what keys are required for each SQL join is crucial to sidestep two primary pitfalls often encountered in data pipelines:

- Generating **unintended duplicates**;
- Trimming the domain of our table, resulting in fewer rows than anticipated. This often occurs when confusing a `LEFT` or `RIGHT` join with an `INNER` join;

The complex part is that employing multiple key joins is not a universally applicable solution. Adding a layer of complexity, there are instances where intentionally generating duplicates may be desirable — consider the next example.

```sql
CREATE TABLE sandbox.unique_customer(
    customer_id INT,
    PRIMARY KEY (customer_id)
);

insert into sandbox.unique_customer (
    customer_id
) values (1), (2), (3);
```

customer_id
1
2
3

Figure 166 – unique_customer table

Suppose we aim to incorporate the monthly balances of these customers into this table. Given that the *customer_unique* table has only one entry per customer, it is logical to perform a join with the customer balance using only the *customer_id*.

```sql
select a.customer_id, b.month, b.balance
from sandbox.unique_customer as a
inner join sandbox.customer_balance as b
on a.customer_id = b.customer_id;
```

customer_id	month	balance
1	201903	10.00
1	201904	15.00
2	201903	1524.00
2	201904	225.00
3	201905	360.00

Figure 167 – Output from multiple key join

To sum up, the realm of table joins in SQL isn't limited to single-key matches—it gracefully extends to multiple-key joins. This widens the scope for merging, manipulating, and analyzing data. **The crucial aspect involves a deep understanding of your data, recognizing specific scenarios, and deploying the most suitable join strategy. The multiplication rule for output table rows stands as a helpful guideline in this context.** Grasping how your keys propagate to the output is mandatory for constructing robust data pipelines.

6.4 Union Operations

Lastly, in the context of combining tables, let's explore the technique of vertically stacking tables. Up to now, we've delved into expanding tables with new columns or refining our output's scope through joins. However, in certain data pipelines, it might be beneficial to stack tables on top of each other when their domains align—this can be achieved with the **UNION** command!

In this example, we'll use data from two fictional "stores", with each store generating a table of invoices.

```
create temporary table sandbox.store_1 (
    invoice_id smallint primary key,
    customer_id smallint,
    item_quantity smallint,
    order_value decimal (19,4),
    product varchar(100)
);

create temporary table sandbox.store_2 (
    invoice_id smallint primary key,
    item_quantity smallint,
    order_value decimal (19,4),
    product varchar(100)
);

# Insert data into Store 1
insert into sandbox.store_1 (
    invoice_id, customer_id, item_quantity,
    order_value, product
) values (123, 10, 100, 20.2, 'Dog Food'), (165, 35, 100,
20.2, 'Cat Food'), (166, 10, 5, 0.95, 'Dog Food');

# Insert data into Store 2
insert into sandbox.store_2 (
    invoice_id, item_quantity,
    order_value, product
) values (652, 15, 18.2, 'Cat Toy'), (685, 50, 21.3, 'Cat
Food');
```

Previewing the tables we've just created:

invoice_id	customer_id	item_quantity	order_value	product
123	10	100	20.2000	Dog Food
165	35	100	20.2000	Cat Food
166	10	5	0.9500	Dog Food

Figure 168 – Store 1 Data

Store 1 has generated 3 invoices, with each invoice containing only one item ordered. In this table we have information about the *invoice_id*, the *customer_id* and the quantity, value and description of the product ordered.

What about the data from store 2? Let's see:

invoice_id	item_quantity	order_value	product
652	15	18.2000	Cat Toy
685	50	21.3000	Cat Food

Figure 169 – Store 2 Data

Notice that our store 2 table has a slightly different structure as we don't have information about the customer who has ordered the product. This difference in the structure of both tables will be important for understanding some key features of the **UNION** command. At our store, we only have two invoices—one for a 'Cat Toy' and another for 'Cat Food.'

If we wanted to combine the data from Store 1 and Store 2, using a join isn't the right approach. Even though there are shared columns between the tables, our goal is not to establish a relationship based on these columns. Instead, we want to stack these tables vertically, and the perfect solution for that is using a **UNION** command!

```sql
select invoice_id, item_quantity, order_value, product
from sandbox.store_1
union
select invoice_id, item_quantity, order_value, product
from sandbox.store_2;
```

The **UNION** command is very simple to understand. Let's break it down into sub-statements, as we've done with other SQL expressions:

- First, we execute a simple SQL **SELECT** statement to fetch everything from the 'store_1' table.
- Next, we perform a **UNION** between both tables — this operation matches the columns from the **SELECT** statement on 'store_1' with the **SELECT** statement on 'store_2'.
- Finally, execute the **SELECT** statement on 'store_2', aligning with the preceding **UNION** command.

The result of the **UNION** operator is a nice looking table with the following look:

invoice_id	item_quantity	order_value	product
123	100	20.2000	Dog Food
165	100	20.2000	Cat Food
166	5	0.9500	Dog Food
652	15	18.2000	Cat Toy
685	50	21.3000	Cat Food

Figure 170 – Output of Union command

Notice, how we've just included the common columns in the **UNION** operation. This is mandatory for **UNION** to work - if you add *customer_id* to the **SELECT** statement we're applying to table 1, you'll see an error.

Apart from this setback, one interesting aspect of the **UNION** operator is its flexibility to combine various select statements when stackomg tables together.. For instance, let's utilize a **WHERE** statement to filter out rows where the item quantity exceeds or is equal to 100 in both tables:

```
select invoice_id, item_quantity, order_value, product
from sandbox.store_1
where item_quantity >= 100
union all
select invoice_id, item_quantity, order_value, product
from sandbox.store_2
where item_quantity >= 100;
```

invoice_id	item_quantity	order_value	product
123	100	20.2000	Dog Food
165	100	20.2000	Cat Food

Figure 171 – Output of Union and Where command

Noticeably, we only include some of the rows from *store_1* in our output since they are the only ones meeting the condition *item_quantity >= 100*. Can you predict the resulting table if we apply the **WHERE** condition to just one side of our **UNION** operation? For instance:

```
select invoice_id, item_quantity, order_value, product
from sandbox.store_1
where item_quantity >= 100
union all
select invoice_id, item_quantity, order_value, product
from sandbox.store_2;
```

invoice_id	item_quantity	order_value	product
123	100	20.2000	Dog Food
165	100	20.2000	Cat Food
652	15	18.2000	Cat Toy
685	50	21.3000	Cat Food

Figure 172 – Output of Union and Where command

Only the rows from *store_1* underwent the filtering process! It's quite interesting to realize that the clauses on either side of the **UNION** operator operate independently.

Recall when I mentioned that the only constraint with **UNION** operators is having identical structures for both tables? Let's explore that by removing certain columns from the **SELECT** statement, arbitrarily.

```
select invoice_id, item_quantity, order_value, product
from sandbox.store_1
where item_quantity >= 100
union all
select invoice_id, item_quantity, order_value
from sandbox.store_2;
```

In the query mentioned above, we are choosing *invoice_id, item_quantity, order_value*, and *product* from *store_1*. However, from *store_2*, we subset different columns and only *invoice_id, item_quantity*, and *order_value* are selected.

Error Code: 1222. The used SELECT statements have a different number of columns

Figure 173 – Error when selecting different columns in the Union operator

We will see an error as the structure of the tables we are trying to combine don't match in the query. Getting the hang of using joins and the **UNION** command is crucial for anyone looking to efficiently work with and analyze data in SQL. This chapter delved into the ins and outs of single-key and multi-key joins, emphasizing the importance of understanding your data and choosing the right join technique. Takeaways from this section are:

- SQL primarily operates by connecting tables through joins, which merge data from different tables based on specified conditions.
- Inner joins combine data where matching values exist in both tables, filtering out rows without corresponding entries in both tables.
- Left joins include all rows from the left table and matching rows from the right table, with **NULL** values for missing matches in the right table.
- Right joins include all rows from the right table and matching rows from the left table, with **NULL** values for missing matches in the left table.
- Multiple key joins involve combining data based on multiple matching columns, offering more precise data integration but requiring careful consideration to avoid unintended duplications.
- The **UNION** operator vertically stacks tables, combining their data, provided that they have identical column structures.
- Understanding the nuances of joins and the **UNION** operator is essential for effective SQL query construction and data analysis.

Now armed with this knowledge, we're all set to tackle the exercises!

6.5 Exercise Section

In this coding exercise section, you will be able to practice what we've learned about combining tables. As usual, let's start by executing a script that will create the tables we will need to query throughout this exercise section:

```sql
CREATE TABLE exercises.records (record_id integer, record_name varchar(50), artist varchar(50), number_tracks integer);

CREATE TABLE exercises.store_stock (store_id integer, record_id integer, stock integer);

CREATE TABLE exercises.stores (store_id integer, store_name varchar(30), manager_name varchar(30));

insert into exercises.records(
    record_id, record_name, artist, number_tracks
    ) values(1, 'Dark Side of the Moon', 'Pink Floyd', 9),
    (2, 'The Raven That Refused to Sing (And Other Stories)', 'Steven Wilson', 6),
    (3, 'Led Zeppelin IV', 'Led Zeppelin', 8),
    (4, 'Menagerie', 'Bill Whiters', 9);

insert into exercises.store_stock(
    store_id, record_id, stock
    ) values
    (1, 1, 10),
    (1, 2, 20),
    (1, 3, 10),
    (2, 2, 12),
    (2, 3, 15),
    (2, 4, 42),
    (3, 1, 30),
    (3, 2, 32);
```

```sql
insert into exercises.stores(
    store_id, record_id, stock
    ) values
    (1, 'Record Club', 'Sammy Gilmour'),
    (2, 'Spin it!', 'Sammy Gilmour'),
    (3, 'The Oak House', 'Jimmy Plant');

CREATE TABLE exercises.la_store_sales (store_id integer,
record_id integer, sold_items integer, price float);

CREATE TABLE exercises.ny_store_sales (store_id integer,
record_id integer, sold_items integer, price float);


insert into exercises.la_store_sales(
    store_id, record_id, sold_items, price
    ) values
    (1, 1, 10, 10.99),
    (2, 1, 5, 11.99),
    (3, 1, 20, 8.99);


insert into exercises.la_store_sales(
    store_id, record_id, sold_items, price
    ) values
    (5, 1, 13, 10.99),
    (6, 1, 52, 11.99),
    (7, 1, 48, 8.99);
```

6.5.1 Exercises

1. Select all rows from the **stores** table and add the column *record_id* and *stock* from the **store_stock** table using *store_id* as key in the join. Retrieve every row from the **stores** table, even if it is not on the **store_stock** table.

2. Select all the rows from the **store_stock** table and add the column *store_name* from the stores table using **store_id** as key in the join. Retrieve only common rows.

3. Sum the stock of each store by its name. Retrieve a table with the following columns:

    - *store_name*

    - *total_stock*, a column containing the total stock of all records of the store.

Note: You'll need to join the stores and store_stock tables.

4. Create a table that contains all the information for both *la* and *ny* stores by combining the tables **la_store_sales** and **ny_store_sales**. Select all the columns from both tables in the process.

5. Create a table that contains all rows for both *la* and *ny* store. Select *store_id*, *record_id* and a calculated column called *revenue* where you multiply the *sold_items* by the *price*

6.5.2 Exercise Solutions

```
1. select a.*, b.store_name from
exercises.store_stock as a
inner join
exercises.stores as b
on a.store_id = b.store_id;

2. select a.*, b.record_id, b.stock from
exercises.stores as a
left join
exercises.store_stock as b
on a.store_id = b.store_id;

3. select a.store_name, sum(b.stock) as total_stock
from exercises.stores as a
inner join exercises.store_stock as b
on a.store_id = b.store_id;

4. select *
from exercises.la_store_sales
union
select *
from exercises.ny_store_sales;

5. select store_id, record_id, sold_items * price as revenue
from exercises.la_store_sales
union
select store_id, record_id, sold_items * price as revenue
from exercises.ny_store_sales;
```

7. More on Select Statements

In these initial 150 pages of this book, we've delved into a variety of aspects concerning SQL queries. Most notably, we've covered some of the key SQL clauses that address a wide range of scenarios for an intermediate SQL user. **By now, you should feel confident in working with SQL, and the knowledge I've shared with you is designed to empower you to handle around 60% to 70% of the typical use cases that most SQL users encounter.**

Now, we're moving into the first section of the book where we'll delve into more advanced concepts. Before diving into this chapter, take a moment to revisit the preceding pages, review the exercises, and make sure you've understood the concepts we've covered thus far. Once you've done that, come back to the checklist below to mark all the topics as clear, and we can continue:

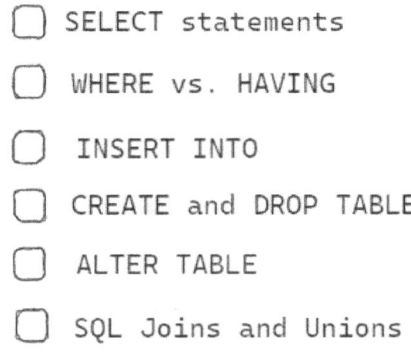

Figure 174 – Checklist of SQL Concepts

After you've become comfortable at working with the concepts above, mark the items as completed. If you can create queries based with these concepts, you're set to move forward with the book. In the upcoming chapter, we will explore two advanced concepts in SQL that will improve your querying abilities:

- **SQL Subqueries:** A subquery, often referred to as a nested query or inner query, allows you to use the result of one query as input of another query. This technique is extremely helpful for more advanced use cases.

- Inserting using `SELECT` statements: This technique is invaluable when you want to insert data from one table into another. Instead of manually inputting data values, you can use a `SELECT` statement to fetch records from an existing table and insert them into a target table.

7.1. Subqueries

It's time to dive into some coding and revisit the famous *sakila* database. Let's kick things off by performing a join to incorporate the *language_id* column into the *sakila.film* table:

```
select a.language_id, b.name, a.length
from sakila.film as a
inner join
sakila.language as b
on a.language_id = b.language_id;
```

Can you guess what the query above returns?

language_id	name	length
1	English	86
1	English	48
1	English	50
1	English	117
1	English	130
1	English	169

Figure 175 – Output from Join between sakila.film and sakila.language

The query provides us with the *id*, *name*, and *length* of the movie. Now, imagine we want to utilize this output for another query, such as calculating the average length of the movies. Would we need to create an additional table in our database for this purpose? No!

We can leverage the concept of subqueries! They represent a powerful concept in SQL, allowing us to work with the tables returned in our queries and nesting them within another statement.

```
select my_query.* from
        (select a.language_id, b.name, a.length
        from sakila.film as a
        inner join
        sakila.language as b
        on a.language_id = b.language_id) as my_query;
```

Although subqueries might seem challenging at first, they're actually quite straightforward. Once you begin visualizing the inner query's output, this concept becomes easy to understand.

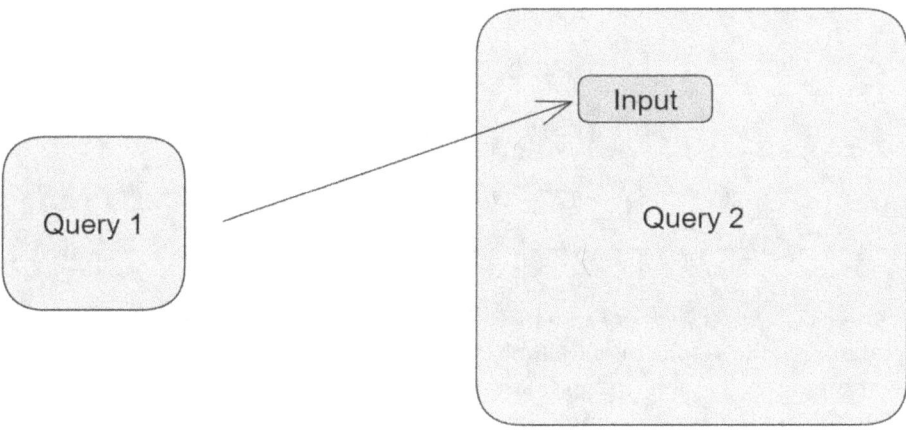

Figure 176 – Diagram of Subqueries

In the code below, we employ a **subquery**, referring to the inner query with an alias named '*my_query*'. Utilizing this alias grants us the flexibility to reference the output as '*my_query*.*' The general form of subqueries is as follows:

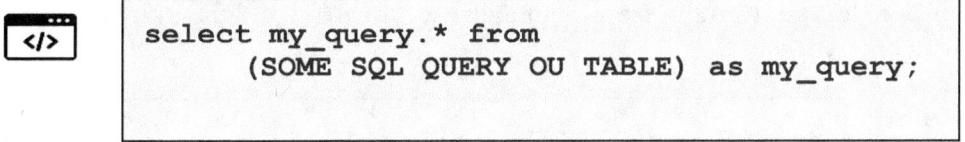
```
select my_query.* from
        (SOME SQL QUERY OU TABLE) as my_query;
```

Utilizing **'select *'** on the result of a query yields the same output as the original query, rendering it redundant. However, subqueries offer possibilities for more complex operations, like computing averages from the values generated by the inner query.

Let's explore this example below:

```
select my_query.name, avg(length) as avg_length
from
        (select a.language_id, b.name, a.length
        from sakila.film as a
        inner join
        sakila.language as b
        on a.language_id = b.language_id) as my_query
group by my_query.name;
```

name	avg_length
▶ English	115.2720

Figure 177 – Output from Sub query

To carry out this calculation, we need to follow a couple of steps:

- Since the *sakila.film* table doesn't include the name of the movie's language, we have to retrieve it from the *sakila.language* table.
- After combining the length and language, we must perform a group-by operation to calculate the average movie length based on the language.

While it's possible to perform this calculation without a subquery, using a subquery in certain instances can improve readability, and provide better opportunities for performance optimization. About the output in Figure 177, here's a question: Can you figure out why we only end up with one row in the resulting table? It's because the *sakila.film* table only contains movies in one language – English!

Subqueries have immense potential as they can enable more complex statements. For instance, let's delve into a double **GROUP BY** example. Initially, we'll extract the total amount spent by each customer with different staff IDs:

```
select customer_id, staff_id,
sum(amount) as total_amount
from sakila.payment
group by 1, 2;
```

This will return a table with the following aspect:

customer_id	staff_id	total_amount
1	1	64.83
1	2	53.85
2	1	60.85
2	2	67.88
3	1	64.86
3	2	70.88

Figure 178 – Customer_id and Staff_id group by example

Analyzing the table in Figure 178, focusing on the first three rows:

- Staff_id 1 has processed $64.83 in purchases from customer id 1.
- Staff_id 2 has processed $53.85 in purchases from customer id 1.
- Staff_id 1 has processed $60.85 in purchases from customer id 2.

Now, consider if we want to determine the count of distinct customers for each *staff_id* in this table. While there's another technique available (**DISTINCT**, a concept we'll discuss shortly), we can also employ another **GROUP BY** on the table using the concept of Subqueries:

```
select staff_id, count(customer_id) as nb_customers
from
(select customer_id, staff_id,
sum(amount) as total_amount
from sakila.payment
group by 1, 2) as summed_customers
group by staff_id;
```

In this scenario, we utilize our primary table as the initial data aggregation point. Based on this output, we determine the count of *customer_ids* attended by each *staff_id*. This is particularly interesting because performing a **GROUP BY** operation directly on the primary table won't yield the desired outcome. This is due to the potential duplication of each *customer_id*, depending on the number of transactions they've conducted in the *sakila.payment* table.

155

Examining the results obtained from the query mentioned above:

staff_id	nb_customers
1	599
2	599

Figure 179 – Number of customers attended by each Staff ID

Based on this, we reach the conclusion that each *staff_id* attended the same number of customers: 599.

In summary, our exploration into coding with the *sakila* database has underscored the significance of subqueries in SQL. Subqueries emerge as a fundamental tool, enabling us to perform complex operations a bit more easily. The examples presented illustrate the versatility and efficacy of this tool in extracting valuable insights from relational databases, although there are myriad other applications to explore that we haven't presented. Also, in handling more complex data structures, subqueries prove to be invaluable allies, emabling us to embed query logic into broader queries.

7.2 Select + Insert Into

SELECT statements open up a range of possibilities beyond their basic use. One such application involves combining **SELECT** statements with **INSERT INTO** statements, providing a new feature in SQL that we haven't explored. Consider a scenario where we want to generate a table containing all the unique first names from our actors. Would we need to manually input them into a **SELECT INTO** clause? Fortunately, no!

Let's start this example by examining the first names in the *sakila.actor* table:

```
SELECT first_name from sakila.actor;
```

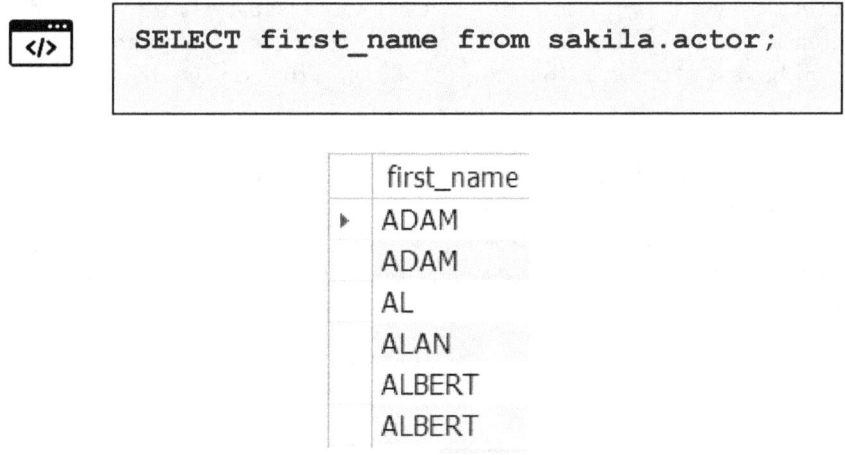

Figure 180 – First names in the sakila.actor table

Notice that we have repeating first names, just as anticipated. For instance, the name "*ADAM*" is listed twice in the *actor* table, corresponding to two actors that share this first name. Our objective is to create a table containing only the unique names and "*ADAM*" must only show up once.

Before going into the combination of **SELECT + INSERT INTO**, let me show you the **DISTINCT** clause, a very cool add on to the **SELECT** statement:

```
SELECT DISTINCT first_name from sakila.actor;
```

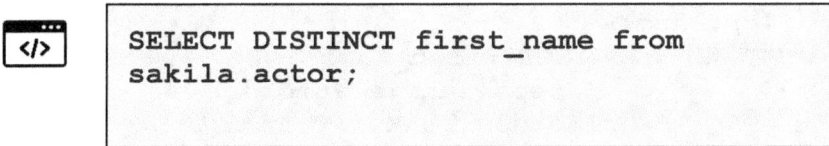

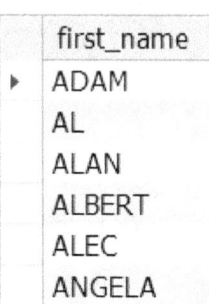

Figure 181 – Distinct First names in the sakila.actor table

Using the "**DISTINCT**" keyword right after the **SELECT** will exclusively retrieve unique values from the table. In our case, we are asking for every distinct *first_name*. If you add more columns to the SELECT when you have a **DISTINCT**, the unique values in the combination of the columns will be retrieved.

Ok, first step done, we have the unique values of first names from the *sakila.actor table*. Now, imagine that we would like to create a new table based on these distinct names. Luckily, we don't have to manually execute an **INSERT INTO** where we write each name *ADAM, AL, ALBERT, ALEC*, etc. We can integrate the results from a **SELECT** statement into an **INSERT INTO** statement by combining both!

As we will want to add this data to a new table, we need to create it using the **CREATE TABLE** command we've already mastered. For this table, we'll opt for a column with *varchar(20)* data type:

```
create table sakila.first_names (
    first_name varchar(20)
    );
```

Right now, *sakila.first_names* is completely empty. Let's populate it with the nice trick that combines **INSERT INTO** and **SELECT**:

```
insert into sakila.first_names (
    first_name
    ) SELECT DISTINCT first_name
                from sakila.actor
                order by first_name;
```

So cool! So, as **SELECT DISTINCT** smartly generates a list with just the first names (the output we've seen in Figure 181), we can feed that result into the **INSERT INTO** statement. This works fine, as we don't need to write the individual rows to add to the table. Take note that when employing these **INSERT INTO** techniques, **it's crucial to respect the constraints of the table we're inserting data into.**

Now, let's take a peek at the contents of *sakila.first_names*:

```
select * from sakila.first_names;
```

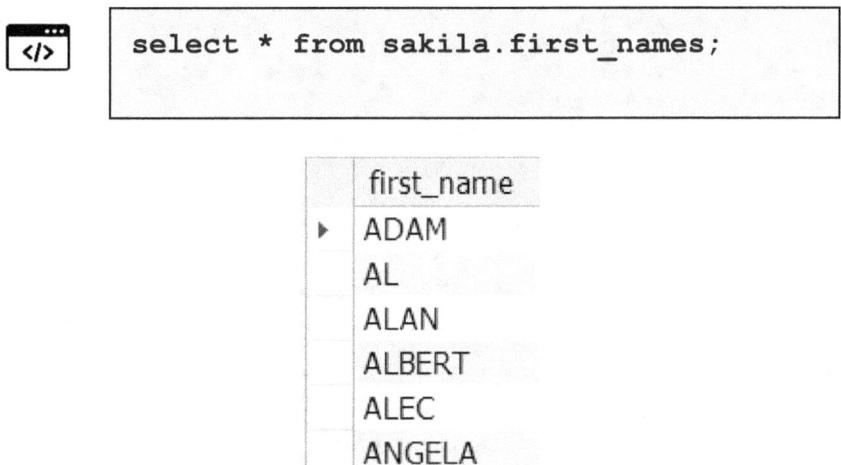

Figure 182 – Distinct First names in the sakila.actor table

sakila.first_names holds the rows from our query result, and we've cleverly sidestepped listing all the names manually in the **INSERT INTO** statement. What's very cool is that we can employ any **SELECT** statement we fancy, as long as the data we're adding aligns with the data types of the columns set to receive it.

Another example would be creating a new table that would only contain "*PG Rated Movies*":

```
create table sakila.pg_movies (
    film_id smallint,
  title varchar(128),
  description text
  );
```

First, we need to filter PG rated movies using a **WHERE** clause:

```
SELECT * FROM
sakila.film
WHERE rating = 'PG';
```

film_id	title	description	release_year	language_id	original_language_id	rental_duration
1	ACADEMY DINOSAUR	A Epic Drama of a Feminist An...	2006	1	NULL	6
6	AGENT TRUMAN	A Intrepid Panorama of a Robo...	2006	1	NULL	3
12	ALASKA PHANTOM	A Fanciful Saga of a Hunter An...	2006	1	NULL	6
13	ALI FOREVER	A Action-Packed Drama of a De...	2006	1	NULL	4
19	AMADEUS HOLY	A Emotional Display of a Pione...	2006	1	NULL	6

Figure 183 – List of PG Rated Movies

This query displays all movies with a *'PG'* rating. Now, we can integrate this with an **INSERT INTO** statement and data into our *pg_movies* table using the knowledge we've gained so far:

```
INSERT INTO sakila.pg_movies (
    film_id, title, description
) SELECT film_id, title, description FROM
sakila.film
WHERE rating = 'PG';
```

It's very nice to see how these SQL concepts intertwine as they fall together on the same principles and ideas. SQL has this ability of combining different concepts into a relative straightforward syntax that is based on a set of common principles.

Now, let's move beyond the theoretical realm and dive into practical coding. Remember that subqueries may seem complex initially, but visualizing the output of the inner query makes them more accessible. Feel free to practice these exercises in chunks as they will guide you through using subqueries effectively and demonstrate their potential for improving query readability.

Time to code!

7.3 Exercise Section

In this coding exercise section, you will be able to practice what we've learned about SQL advanced topics until now. As usual, let's start by executing a script that will create the table we will need to query throughout this exercise section.

```sql
CREATE TABLE exercises.transactions (store_id integer,
employee_id integer, customer_id integer, total_value
float);

CREATE TABLE exercises.employees (employee_id integer,
employee_full_name varchar(40));

CREATE TABLE exercises.customers (customer_id integer,
customer_full_name varchar(40));

insert into exercises.transactions(
    store_id, employee_id, customer_id, total_value
    ) values(1, 1, 2, 10.5),
    (1, 1, 2, 20),
    (1, 1, 1, 18),
    (1, 2, 2, 25),
    (1, 3, 1, 27),
    (1, 2, 3, 19),
    (1, 2, 4, 29);

insert into exercises.employees(
    employee_id, employee_full_name
    ) values
    (1, "Richerd Richard"),
    (2, "May May"),
    (3, "Anne Anne");
```

7.3.1 Exercises

1. Count the number of distinct customers that each employee assisted. Notice that one employee might attend the same customer on the *transactions* table multiple times. You can use a subquery and a double group by for the effect. The output table should have an *employee_id* and a *count_customers* column.

2. Select the distinct number of stores in the transactions table. The output table should only have one column: *store_id*

3. Insert into the *customers* table all customers that have done transactions. The customers table only has a single column, *customer_*id.

4. Insert into the customers table the customers that have done transactions on store_id number 2. Note: The customers table should have only one line per customer. The customers table only has a single column, customer_id.

7.3.2 Exercise Solutions

1. ```
   select employee_id, count(customer_id) as count_customers
       from (
       select employee_id, customer_id, count(*) as count_cust
       from exercises.transactions
       group by employee_id, customer_id
       )
       group by employee_id;
   ```

2. ```
   select distinct store_id
       from exercises.transactions;
   ```

3. ```
   insert into customers_val (
     customer_id
     ) select distinct customer_id
       from exercises.transactions;
   ```

4. ```
   insert into customers_val (
     customer_id
     ) select distinct customer_id
       from exercises.transactions
       where store_id = 2;
   ```

8 Updating Information

Once we've established our own tables, the next step is to update the information they hold without encountering any restrictions. If the data we inserted into the table were static, the utility of SQL would be considerably poor, **as it would persistently store every type of data added to our tables, preventing us from changing.** Updating data within our tables becomes achievable by employing a combination of a group of clauses known as **UPDATE-SET-WHERE**. The integration of these three statements enables us to modify any data of our tables based on specific conditions.

8.1 Update – Set – Where

To illustrate, let's start by creating a table featuring various students' relevant information such as birthday date or their favourite class:

```sql
create table sandbox.students (
    student_id integer,
    student_full_name varchar(40) not null,
    birth_date date,
    favorite_class varchar(40)
);

insert into sandbox.students (
    student_id, student_full_name, birth_date,
favorite_class
    ) values (1, 'Joe Doe', '2000-04-03', 'History'),
             (2, 'Mary Doe', '2000-06-02', 'Mathematics'),
             (3, 'John Smith', '2000-02-10', 'English'),
             (4, 'Anne Smith', '2000-01-02', 'Mathematics'),
             (5, 'May John', '2000-06-06', 'History');
```

Let's check a preview of our students table:

student_id	student_full_name	birth_date	favorite_class
1	Joe Doe	2000-04-03	History
2	Mary Doe	2000-06-02	Mathematics
3	John Smith	2000-02-10	English
4	Anne Smith	2000-01-02	Mathematics
5	May John	2000-06-06	History

Figure 184 – Students table

The *students* table contains details about a group of students:

- *Student_id*: Identifying number assigned to each student (integer).
- *Student_full_name*: Full name, including both first and last names.
- *Birth_date*: Date of birth for the student.
- *Favorite_class*: The student's preferred class.

Now, let's picture that our students would look into this table and notice some inaccuracies. For example, *Mary John's* favorite class is being incorrectly listed as History when, in reality, she has a keen interest in Mathematics. How can we rectify this without resorting to the time-consuming process of deleting and reinserting all the rows? Enter the `UPDATE SET WHERE` sequence.

Note: Before proceeding, we'll need to adjust the `SQL_SAFE_UPDATES` to 0: `SET SQL_SAFE_UPDATES = 0;`

With this in place, let's use a new clause to update Mary John's favorite class to Mathematics:

```
UPDATE sandbox.students
SET favorite_class = "Mathematics"
WHERE student_id = 5;
```

Let's break down our instructions step by step:

- First, we use `'update sandbox.students'` to specify the table we want to update.
- Next, we employ `set favorite_class = 'Mathematics'` to indicate the value we want to update in our table. In this instance, we're specifying that the values in the `'favorite_class'` column should be changed to `'Mathematics'`.
- Finally, we outline all the scenarios where this column should be updated. Here, the `'where'` clause acts as a guardrail, ensuring the condition is met, and we only update this column for cases where `'student_id = 5'`.

Running this query will perform its wonders on our table:

student_id	student_full_name	birth_date	favorite_class
1	Joe Doe	2000-04-03	History
2	Mary Doe	2000-06-02	Mathematics
3	John Smith	2000-02-10	English
4	Anne Smith	2000-01-02	Mathematics
5	May John	2000-06-06	Mathematics

Figure 185 – Updated Students Table

As usual, you know what's cool with the **UPDATE-SET-WHERE** logic? Everything we've leaned about table structures and the application of **WHERE** statements comes into play here!

For instance, we can modify values in our table by applying a condition involving multiple statements. An illustration would be attempting to update the *favorite_class* of several students at the same time, such as "*Joe Doe*" and "*John Smith*":

```
update sandbox.students
set favorite_class = "Arts"
where student_full_name = 'Joe Doe' or student_full_name
= 'John Smith';
```

The structure of our **WHERE** clause resembles the other **OR** clauses we've employed previously. This is quite impressive, as it enables the simultaneous update of both records for "*Joe Doe*" and "*John Smith*" in a single query.

student_id	student_full_name	birth_date	favorite_class
1	Joe Doe	2000-04-03	Arts
2	Mary Doe	2000-06-02	Mathematics
3	John Smith	2000-02-10	Arts
4	Anne Smith	2000-01-02	Mathematics
5	May John	2000-06-06	Mathematics

Figure 186 – Updated Students Table

However, similar to our previous statements in SQL, it is imperative that all statements adhere to the established conditions within our tables. Take, for instance, the *student_id*, a key in our table, which cannot be **NULL**. Let's attempt to modify this column for a particular student and set it to **NULL**, seeing if that works:

```
update sandbox.students
set student_full_name = NULL
where student_id = 1;
```

Unfortunately, this will result in an error – let's confirm that:

Error Code: 1048. Column 'student_full_name' cannot be null

Figure 187 – Error in Updating Sandbox.students

The SQL error code is straightforward - it states that "*student_full_name*" cannot be null, preventing us from executing the update in the table. Moreover, we have the capability to execute multiple updates on distinct columns simultaneously. Consider a scenario where we desire to modify both the "*student_full_name*" to "John" and the favorite class to *Mathematics* for the student with *student_id = 1*. This can be achieved with the following query:

```
update sandbox.students
set student_full_name = "John", favorite_class = "Mathematics"
where student_id = 1;
```

Take note that when updating multiple columns simultaneously, we don't employ the connector "**AND**". Instead, we utilize a comma to separate the various columns that we want for update. This represents a distinctive scenario, and we need to be careful consideration when changing multiple columns. Now, let's examine the resulting set returned by the aforementioned query:

student_id	student_full_name	birth_date	favorite_class
1	John	2000-04-03	Mathematics
2	Mary Doe	2000-06-02	Mathematics
3	John Smith	2000-02-10	Arts
4	Anne Smith	2000-01-02	Mathematics
5	May John	2000-06-06	Mathematics

Figure 188 – Updated Students Table

An important note – we need to be extremely careful when dealing with update statements, especially those lacking **WHERE** clauses! Let's explore the consequences that show up when the **WHERE** clause is inadvertently overlooked in the UPDATE statement.

```
update sandbox.students
set student_full_name = "John";
```

student_id	student_full_name	birth_date	favorite_class
1	John	2000-04-03	Mathematics
2	John	2000-06-02	Mathematics
3	John	2000-02-10	Arts
4	John	2000-01-02	Mathematics
5	John	2000-06-06	Mathematics

Figure 189 – Updated Students Table

Regrettably, the absence of a **WHERE** clause will result in the update of the column value for all rows. This poses a significant risk and is a common error made by many individuals when attempting to update values in tables.

Mastering the **UPDATE-SET-WHERE** sequence is essential for modifying data within our tables. As we delve into the detail of this trio of statements, we gain the ability to make targeted updates based on specific conditions, preventing the need for time-consuming deletion and reinsertion processes. Furthermore, the capability to execute multiple updates simultaneously adds a layer of efficiency to our data management processes.

8.2 Exercises

In this coding exercise section, you will be able to practice what we've learned about updating information in SQL. As usual, let's start by executing a script that will create the table we will need to query throughout this exercise section.

```
create table exercises.students (
      student_id integer auto_increment primary key,
    student_full_name varchar(30),
    favorite_classes varchar(150),
    student_age integer,
    birth_date date,
    degree varchar(30)
    );

insert into exercises.students (
      student_full_name, favorite_classes, student_age,
birth_date, degree
) values ('John Smith', 'Mathematics, Political Science,
Biology', 23, '1999-03-01', 'Engineering'),
      ('Amy Smith', 'History, Political Science, Biology',
23, '1999-03-01', 'History'),
      ('Joe Adams', 'History, Mathematics', 23, '1999-06-01',
'History'),
      ('Joe Williams', 'Biology, Chemistry', 22, '2000-03-01',
'Chemistry'),
      ('Anne Williams', 'Mathematics, Arts', 22, '2000-03-16',
'Mathematics'),
      ('May Taylor', 'History, Geography', 22, '2000-05-19',
'History'),
      ('Zoe Brown', 'Physical Education, History', 21, '2001-
02-18', 'Physical Education'),
      ('Jennifer Davies', 'Biology, Chemistry', 21, '2001-03-
19', 'Chemistry'),
      ('Robert Jones', 'Chemistry, Biology, Mathematics', 21,
'2001-06-02', 'Chemistry');      (3, "Anne Anne");
```

8.2.1 Exercise

1. Update the degree of the student with the full name "John Smith" to "Chemistry"

2. Update the *favorite_classes* of the students with degree "Chemistry" and 21 years old to "Chemistry, Science"

3. Update the *birth_date* of the students with *student_id* 1 or 2 to '2001-01-01'

4. Update the age and degree to 19 and "Arts" of students with the id 1 or 4.

8.2.2 Exercise Solutions

```
1 update exercises.students
set degree = 'Chemistry'
where student_full_name = 'John Smith';

2. update exercises.students
set favorite_classes = 'Chemistry, Science'
where degree = 'Chemistry' and student_age = 21;

3. update exercises.students
set birth_date = '2001-01-01'
where student_id in (1, 2);

4. update exercises.students
set degree = 'Arts', student_age = 19
where student_id in (1,4);
```

9 Advanced Filtering

During the past chapters, you've seen how important the **WHERE** clause is, in the context of SQL programming. We were able to discuss several topics on typical filtering operations and how we can leverage mathematical or logical operators for more efficient data manipulation.

But, the flexibility of the **WHERE** clause does not stop in those simpler use cases! This operator contains some other advanced clauses that we can leverage for complex filters. In this chapter, we'll delve into some of them: The Not Operator, Operator Precedence and Wildcards.

9.1 The Not Operator

For this subchapter, we'll need to create a new version of the students table with more examples of students' data. Before proceeding, run the following code:

```
drop table sandbox.students;

create table sandbox.students (
        student_id integer auto_increment primary key,
    student_full_name varchar(30),
    favorite_classes varchar(150),
    student_age integer,
    birth_date date,
    degree varchar(30)
    );

insert into sandbox.students (
        student_full_name, favorite_classes, student_age, birth_date, degree
) values ('John Smith', 'Mathematics, Political Science, Biology', 23, '1999-03-01', 'Engineering'),
        ('Amy Smith', 'History, Political Science, Biology', 23, '1999-03-01', 'History'),
    ('Joe Adams', 'History, Mathematics', 23, '1999-06-01', 'History'),
    ('Joe Williams', 'Biology, Chemistry', 22, '2000-03-01', 'Chemistry'),
    ('Anne Williams', 'Mathematics, Arts', 22, '2000-03-16', 'Mathematics'),
    ('May Taylor', 'History, Geography', 22, '2000-05-19', 'History'),
    ('Zoe Brown', 'Physical Education, History', 21, '2001-02-18', 'Physical Education'),
    ('Jennifer Davies', 'Biology, Chemistry', 21, '2001-03-19', 'Chemistry'),
    ('Robert Jones', 'Chemistry, Biology, Mathematics', 21, '2001-06-02', 'Chemistry');
```

In chapter 3.2, we've checked the interesting IN operator that enabled us to select multiple elements at the same time. Don't recall it? I've got you covered:

```
select * from sandbox.students
where student_full_name IN ('Joe Adams','John
Smith','Amy Smith');
```

In the code we see above, we are selecting data from our table where the student's fullname is "Joe Adams", "John Smith" or "Amy Smith".

student_id	student_full_name	favorite_classes	student_age	birth_date	degree
1	John Smith	Mathematics, Political Science, Biology	23	1999-03-01	Engineering
2	Amy Smith	History, Political Science, Biology	23	1999-03-01	History
3	Joe Adams	History, Mathematics	23	1999-06-01	History
NULL	NULL	NULL	NULL	NULL	NULL

Figure 190 – IN Selection (Joe Adams, John Smith, Amy Smith)

In SQL, we can also perform a "not including" clause using the keyword **NOT**. In our example, this will subset all students that are not named "John Smith", nor "Amy Smith" or "Joe Adams" therefore including all other students in the resulting set.

Let's see:

```
select * from sandbox.students
where student_full_name NOT IN ('Joe Adams','John
Smith','Amy Smith');
```

student_id	student_full_name	favorite_classes	student_age	birth_date	degree
4	Joe Williams	Biology, Chemistry	22	2000-03-01	Chemistry
5	Anne Williams	Mathematics, Arts	22	2000-03-16	Mathematics
6	May Taylor	History, Geography	22	2000-05-19	History
7	Zoe Brown	Physical Education, History	21	2001-02-18	Physical Education
8	Jennifer Davies	Biology, Chemistry	21	2001-03-19	Chemistry
9	Robert Jones	Chemistry, Biology, Mathematics	21	2001-06-02	Chemistry
NULL	NULL	NULL	NULL	NULL	NULL

Figure 191 – NOT IN Selection (Joe Adams, John Smith, Amy Smith)

The **NOT** clause is extremely powerful as it can be used with a multitude of other clauses in **WHERE** statements. Let's analyze the following query:

```
select * from sandbox.students
where student_age = 22 and NOT student_full_name =
'Joe Williams';
```

In this case, we are retrieving two subsets of students:

- Students not named "Joe Williams"
- Students that are 22 years old.

Notice how the **AND** clause connects both statements? This means that if there is a 22 year old student named "Joe Williams", it will not show up in the resulting set. Not is effectively negating all cases where the student's name is "Joe Williams", even if it matches the first condition (student is 22 years old).

You can use NOT with every filtering condition we've seen so far. Can you experiment with this clause in other queries we've developed and see how it impacts the resulting set?

9.2 Order of Operations

With new clauses to use in the **WHERE** operator we also open the possibilities for complex or convoluted filtering statements. Luckily, there's some rules that we can apply to help us understand our queries a bit better. For example, let's check the following query:

```
select * from sandbox.students
where degree = 'Chemistry' OR student_age = 23 AND
favorite_classes = 'History, Mathematics';
```

We have three conditions in our **WHERE** clause:

- Student degree is equal to "Chemistry".
- Student is 23 years old.
- Favorite classes are History and Mathematics.

Now, notice the connectors of these clauses. The first two clauses are connected by an **OR** clause while the last two are connected by an **AND**. Does this mean that we are retrieving the following?

- I want all students that have a chemistry degree or are 23. Additionally, their favorite classes must be History and Mathematics

What do you think?

Unfortunately, no! Because of a SQL rule called **order of operator.** This dictates how the clauses align within the **WHERE** statement. Mostly, it words as follows:

- Rule 1: AND clauses have a priority over OR clauses.
- Rule 2: Rule 1 can be overriden by using parenthesis.

In this case, our clause is working in the following way:

- I want all students that have a chemistry degree. Additionally, I want to subset all 23 year old students whose favorite classes are History and Mathematics.

Let's see that in the output:

student_id	student_full_name	favorite_classes	student_age	birth_date	degree
3	Joe Adams	History, Mathematics	23	1999-06-01	History
4	Joe Williams	Biology, Chemistry	22	2000-03-01	Chemistry
8	Jennifer Davies	Biology, Chemistry	21	2001-03-19	Chemistry
9	Robert Jones	Chemistry, Biology, Mathematics	21	2001-06-02	Chemistry

Figure 192 – NOT IN Selection with AND clause

As you can see all students respect the condition stated. Apart from the Chemistry students, we have a single student not belonging to that degree and guess what.. it's a 23 year old with History and Mathematics as favorite classes! But, what happens if we add parenthesis to this **WHERE** clause?

```
select * from sandbox.students
where (degree = 'Chemistry' OR student_age = 23) AND
favorite_classes = 'History, Mathematics';
```

student_id	student_full_name	favorite_classes	student_age	birth_date	degree
3	Joe Adams	History, Mathematics	23	1999-06-01	History

Figure 193 – NOT IN Selection using Parenthesis

The result is totally different! Right now, we are asking for:

- I want all students that have a chemistry degree and are 23 years old. Additionally, I want to subset all students whose favorite classes are History and Mathematics.

As no Chemistry student is 23 in our dataset, the only student returned on this new query is *"Joe Adams"*. The conditions inside the parenthesis are now evaluated together, contrary to what happened in the previous query.

With this knowledge can you guess the output of the following examples? Write the expected output down before taking a peek at the real result on the figures!

```
select * from sandbox.students
where (degree = 'Chemistry' OR student_age = 23 OR
student_full_name = 'May Taylor')
AND student_id > 3;
```

student_id	student_full_name	favorite_classes	student_age	birth_date	degree
4	Joe Williams	Biology, Chemistry	22	2000-03-01	Chemistry
6	May Taylor	History, Geography	22	2000-05-19	History
8	Jennifer Davies	Biology, Chemistry	21	2001-03-19	Chemistry
9	Robert Jones	Chemistry, Biology, Mathematics	21	2001-06-02	Chemistry

Figure 194 – Operator Precedence Example

In this case, here's what we are returning in the output:

- I want all students that are majoring in Chemistry or are 23 or are named *May Taylor*.
- Additionally, we need the students returned above to have *student_id* over 3.

Let's look to another example:

```
select * from sandbox.students
where (degree = 'John Smith' AND student_age = 23)
AND degree = 'History';
```

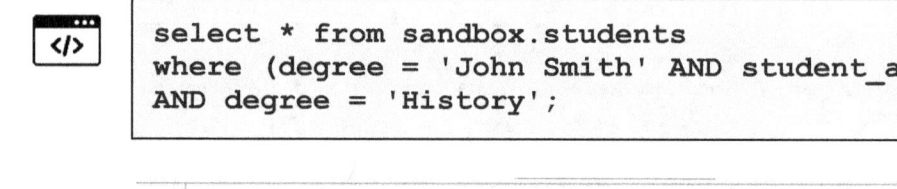

Figure 195 – Operator Precedence Example

In this last example, here's what we are returning in the output:

- I want all students that are named *John Smith* and are 23.
- Additionally, we need those students to have a degree in *History*.

As no students match these conditions, we have an empty resulting set.

In conclusion, understanding the order of operations in SQL **WHERE** clauses is crucial for accurately filtering data according to our criteria. By grasping concepts like the priority of **AND** over **OR** clauses and the use of parentheses to override default precedence, we gain clarity on how our queries are interpreted by the database engine. With practice and experimentation, we can sharpen our skills in crafting effective SQL queries, ensuring that we retrieve the desired data consistently. Take a moment to predict the output based on the order of operations, honing your understanding of SQL logic and enhancing your proficiency in database querying. Make sure that you experiment with different **WHERE** clauses by writing down the output before running your queries. Also, I've got you covered as you'll have the opportunity to explore this concept a bit later in our usual exercise section!

9.3 Wildcards

In SQL, wildcards serve as powerful tools for filtering data based on specific patterns or subsets within a dataset. They allow for flexible and dynamic querying, enabling users to match patterns within text or string data. In this chapter, we'll delve into the concept of wildcards and explore how they can be effectively utilized in SQL queries.

Wildcards revolve around three fundamental elements:

- The **LIKE** clause
- The '**%**' character
- The '**_**' character

These elements form the cornerstone of wildcard functionality, enabling users to create interesting filtering conditions tailored to their specific requirements. Let's start by looking into the **LIKE** clause that serves as the gateway to wildcard functionality. This allows users to specify patterns to match within text or string data. The '**%**' and '**_**' characters are integral components of the **LIKE** clause, facilitating pattern matching operations.

LIKE combines with the '**%**' character, that functions as a placeholder for any sequence of characters. The combination of the two enables users to match patterns based on varying prefixes, suffixes, or substrings within the data.

```
SELECT * FROM sandbox.students
WHERE student_full_name LIKE '%Smith';
```

In this example, the '**%**' character signifies that any sequence of characters preceding the term "Smith" is acceptable. Thus, the query retrieves all rows where the full name ends with "**Smith**" regardless of what precedes it.

student_id	student_full_name	favorite_classes	student_age	birth_date	degree
1	John Smith	Mathematics, Political Science, Biology	23	1999-03-01	Engineering
2	Amy Smith	History, Political Science, Biology	23	1999-03-01	History
NULL	NULL	NULL	NULL	NULL	NULL

Figure 196 – "Smith" last name query result

Can you guess how we can use wildcards to search for all students whose first name is Joe? Let's see:

```
SELECT * FROM sandbox.students
WHERE student_full_name LIKE 'Joe%';
```

student_id	student_full_name	favorite_classes	student_age	birth_date	degree
3	Joe Adams	History, Mathematics	23	1999-06-01	History
4	Joe Williams	Biology, Chemistry	22	2000-03-01	Chemistry
NULL	NULL	NULL	NULL	NULL	NULL

Figure 197 – "Joe" first name query result

Here, the '%' character is positioned after "Joe" indicating that any characters following "Joe" are acceptable.

Another alternative is to use wildcards on both sides of the characters to search:

```
SELECT * FROM sandbox.students
WHERE student_full_name LIKE '%am%';
```

student_id	student_full_name	favorite_classes	student_age	birth_date	degree
2	Amy Smith	History, Political Science, Biology	23	1999-03-01	History
3	Joe Adams	History, Mathematics	23	1999-06-01	History
4	Joe Williams	Biology, Chemistry	22	2000-03-01	Chemistry
5	Anne Williams	Mathematics, Arts	22	2000-03-16	Mathematics
NULL	NULL	NULL	NULL	NULL	NULL

Figure 198 – Names that contain "am" query

By placing the '%' character on both sides of "am," this query identifies all rows containing "am" anywhere within the full name.

In contrast to the '%' character's broad matching capability, the '_' character serves a more precise role. It represents a single character placeholder within the pattern, allowing users to specify exact positions for matching characters or substrings. For example, if we want to retrieve all students that have an "o" as the second letter of their name, we can use the following:

```
SELECT * FROM sandbox.students
WHERE student_full_name LIKE '_o%';
```

student_id	student_full_name	favorite_classes	student_age	birth_date	degree
1	John Smith	Mathematics, Political Science, Biology	23	1999-03-01	Engineering
3	Joe Adams	History, Mathematics	23	1999-06-01	History
4	Joe Williams	Biology, Chemistry	22	2000-03-01	Chemistry
7	Zoe Brown	Physical Education, History	21	2001-02-18	Physical Education
9	Robert Jones	Chemistry, Biology, Mathematics	21	2001-06-02	Chemistry
NULL	NULL	NULL	NULL	NULL	NULL

Figure 199 – Names that contain "o" as the second letter query

In this example, the '_' character precedes "o," indicating that any single character can occupy the position before "o" This query selects all rows where the second character of the full name is "o" like "John", "Joe", "Zoe" or "Robert".

Wildcards serve as indispensable instruments for constructing dynamic SQL queries. Through the adept utilization of the **LIKE** clause alongside the versatile '%' and '_' characters, users gain the ability to sift through data, targeting distinct patterns or subsets within their datasets. Embracing the experimentation of wildcards within SQL queries expands one's repertoire of data manipulation techniques, particularly when it comes to increasingly complex filter.

9.3 Exercises

In this coding exercise section, you will be able to practice what we've learned about the **NOT** operator, order of operations and Wildcards. If you didn't run the **students** table in the previous exercise section, feel free to run it here:

```
create table exercises.students (
      student_id integer auto_increment primary key,
   student_full_name varchar(30),
   favorite_classes varchar(150),
   student_age integer,
   birth_date date,
   degree varchar(30)
   );

insert into exercises.students (
      student_full_name, favorite_classes, student_age,
birth_date, degree
) values ('John Smith', 'Mathematics, Political Science, Biology',
23, '1999-03-01', 'Engineering'),
        ('Amy Smith', 'History, Political Science, Biology', 23,
'1999-03-01', 'History'),
     ('Joe Adams', 'History, Mathematics', 23, '1999-06-01',
'History'),
     ('Joe Williams', 'Biology, Chemistry', 22, '2000-03-01',
'Chemistry'),
     ('Anne Williams', 'Mathematics, Arts', 22, '2000-03-16',
'Mathematics'),
     ('May Taylor', 'History, Geography', 22, '2000-05-19',
'History'),
     ('Zoe Brown', 'Physical Education, History', 21, '2001-02-18',
'Physical Education'),
     ('Jennifer Davies', 'Biology, Chemistry', 21, '2001-03-19',
'Chemistry'),
     ('Robert Jones', 'Chemistry, Biology, Mathematics', 21, '2001-
06-02', 'Chemistry');     (3, "Anne Anne");
```

9.3.1 Exercise

1. Select all students whose name is not "John Smith". Make sure you use the NOT syntax. Select all columns.

2. Select all students that have a degree in History and that are not named "Amy Smith". Make sure you use the NOT syntax. Select all columns.

3. Select all students that have a degree in History and that are not 23 years old or students that have a degree in Mathematics. Select all columns.

4. Select all students whose first name is "Amy". Select all columns.

5. Select all students whose degree contains an 'h' as the second letter. Select all columns.

9.3.2 Exercise Solutions

```
1 select * from
Exercises.students
where not student_full_name = 'John Smith';

2. select * from
exercises.students
where degree = 'History' and not student_full_name = 'Amy Smith';

3. select * from
exercises.students
where (degree = 'History' and not student_age = 23) or degree =
'Mathematics';

4. select * from
exercises.students
where student_full_name LIKE 'Amy%';
```

```
5. select * from
exercises.students
where degree LIKE '_h%';
```

10 Conclusion

Wow, that was cool. From the foundational stages of setting up MySQL Server, Shell, and Workbench to the details of query formulation and data manipulation, each chapter of this book has unfolded a new dimension, enriching your expertise in managing relational databases effectively.

We've come a long way as our journey started with the setup of MySQL, laying the groundwork for the exploration that followed. We navigated through the labyrinth of query basics, mastering the art of filtering, sorting, and extracting insights from vast datasets. As we progressed, we delved into the realm of table creation and modification, understanding the importance of database design in ensuring efficiency and scalability. We understood the complexities of combining tables through various join operations, empowering us to merge datasets seamlessly and extract meaningful correlations. Finally, we checked advanced filtering techniques that have expanded our toolkit, enabling us to refine queries with precision using wildcard characters, order of operations, and the strategic use of the NOT operator.

However, the culmination of this journey does not mark an endpoint in your quest for SQL knowledge. As you say goodbye to these pages, I urge you to carry forward the torch of curiosity and continue our pursuit of excellence in learning more about this great language. In the ever-evolving landscape of technology, the significance of proficient database management cannot be overstated. Whether you are an enthusiast embarking on your journey or a seasoned professional seeking to refine your skills, **remember that mastery is a continuous journey, fueled by passion, perseverance, and a commitment to lifelong learning.**

Furthermore, exploring advanced topics in data analytics and business intelligence (BI) can unlock new possibilities for leveraging data to drive strategic decision-making within organizations. Familiarizing yourself with tools and frameworks such as Tableau, Power BI, or Apache Spark can empower you to extract actionable insights from complex datasets and communicate findings effectively. Also, staying keeping track of emerging trends and technologies in the field of database management, such as cloud-based databases, NoSQL databases, and blockchain-based databases, can position you at the forefront of innovation and give you with the tools to tackle tomorrow's challenges head-on.

Ok, I'll head off but one last recommendation: don't underestimate the value of continuous practice and hands-on experimentation. Building real-world projects, participating in online communities and forums, and seeking out mentorship opportunities can provide invaluable practical experience and foster a supportive network of peers and experts.

In closing, I want to thank you for taking the time to read this book and go through these pages. It really means the world to me. Thank you for joining me on this odyssey through MySQL and it has been a privilege to accompany you on this journey. Feel free to send me feedback on LinkedIn or to my email address **ivo@daredata.engineering** – it will be especially helpful to improve exercises and the flow of the book.

Until we meet again, may your databases be optimized, your queries be swift, and your journey towards MySQL mastery be filled with boundless exploration and success!

Happy querying!

About the Author

Ivo Bernardo is a professional with a passion for Data Science and Analytics, currency a Partner at DareData Engineering, a startup that implements machine learning systems all around the world for companies of different sizes (from startups to large enterprises).

He holds a master Degree in Statistics and Business Intelligence from New University of Lisbon (NOVA IMS) and has been an instructor in several data science academies throughout the years. His main teaching passion is helping beginners or professionals from other industries take their first leap into the Data Science and Analytics space.

Technically he has worked with Python, R, SQL and main cloud providers' infrastructure, developing machine learning models and setting up data science and analytics systems.

You can find him on LinkedIn (https://www.linkedin.com/in/ivobernardo/), Udemy (https://www.udemy.com/user/ivo-bernardo/) or Medium (https://ivopbernardo.medium.com/).

www.ingramcontent.com/pod-product-compliance
Lightning Source LLC
Chambersburg PA
CBHW062104220526
45471CB00010B/3594